Insurance Law in Latvia

Insurance Law in Latvia

Vadim Mantrov

This book was originally published as a monograph in the International Encyclopaedia of Laws/Insurance Law.

Founding Editor: Roger Blanpain
General Editor: Frank Hendrickx
Volume Editor: Herman Cousy

Wolters Kluwer

Published by:
Kluwer Law International B.V.
PO Box 316
2400 AH Alphen aan den Rijn
The Netherlands
E-mail: international-sales@wolterskluwer.com
Website: lrus.wolterskluwer.com

Sold and distributed in North, Central and South America by:
Wolters Kluwer Legal & Regulatory U.S.
7201 McKinney Circle
Frederick, MD 21704
United States of America
Email: customer.service@wolterskluwer.com

Sold and distributed in all other countries by:
Air Business Subscriptions
Rockwood House
Haywards Heath
West Sussex
RH16 3DH
United Kingdom
Email: international-customerservice@wolterskluwer.com

Printed on acid-free paper

ISBN 978-94-035-0523-7

e-Book: ISBN 978-94-035-0524-4
web-PDF: ISBN 978-94-035-0525-1

Printed in the United Kingdom.

The Author

Dr iur. Vadim Mantrov is Docent of Civil Law and Research Fellow at the Faculty of Law, University of Latvia; he is also the Head of the Legal Science Institute of the Faculty. He is appointed and reappointed as an expert in legal science by the Latvian Council of Science since 2012 for the maximum three-year term (2012–2015, 2015–2018, 2018–2021).

He is an author or a co-author for more than fifty scientific publications, including individual and collective monographs, in Latvian, English and Russian. His authored monograph published by Springer was recognised as one of eleven scientific achievements in the Latvian science in 2015 by the Latvian Academy of Sciences.

He has participated in several significant international and domestic scientific projects. He has delivered papers on topical civil law issues in more than thirty international and domestic scientific conferences in Latvia and other European countries as well as in Russia.

His main research interests are related to civil law, covering risk regulation, quality product protection, relationship between general civil law and special civil law branches such as insurance law, consumer protection, intellectual property and regulation of competition relationships.

The Author

Table of Contents

List of Abbreviations

Cabinet	Cabinet of Ministers of the Republic of Latvia (*Latvijas Republikas Ministru kabinets* in Latvian)
CJEU	Court of Justice of the European Union, this term also covers the previous title of the court, i.e., European Court of Justice
Codifying Motor Insurance Directive	Directive 2009/103/EC of the European Parliament and of the Council of 16 September 2009 relating to insurance against civil liability in respect of the use of motor vehicles, and the enforcement of the obligation to insure against such liability. Official Journal, L 263, 07.10.2009, pp. 11–31
Commercial Act	Commercial Law (*Komerclikums* in Latvian)
Consumer Rights Protection Act	Consumer Rights Protection Law (*Patērētāju tiesību aizsardzības likums* in Latvian)
EC	European Community
EEC	European Economic Community
EEZ	European Economic Zone
EU	European Union
FKTK	Financial and Capital Market Commission (*Finanšu un kapitāla tirgus komisija* in Latvian)
Insurance and Reinsurance Act	Insurance and Reinsurance Law (*Apdrošināšanas un pārapdrošināšanas likums* in Latvian)
Insurance and Reinsurance Intermediaries Activity Act (IRIAA)	Activities of Insurance and Reinsurance Intermediaries Law (*Apdrošināšanas un pārapdrošināšanas starpnieku darbības likums* in Latvian)
Insurance Contract Act (ICA)	Law 'On Insurance Contracts' (*Likums 'Par apdrošināšanas līgumu'* in Latvian)

List of Abbreviations

Latvian Civil Act (CL)	Civil Law of the Republic of Latvia of the year 1937 (*Latvijas Republikas 1937.gada Civillikums* in Latvian)[1]
Latvian Supreme Court	Supreme Court of the Republic of Latvia (*Latvijas Republikas Augstākā tiesa* in Latvian), by covering any department of this court
Liability Insurance	Civil Liability Insurance
Motor Insurance	Compulsory Civil Liability Insurance of Motor Vehicles' Drivers
Motor Insurance Act (MIA)	Compulsory Civil Liability Insurance of Owners of Motor Vehicles Law (*Sauszemes transportlīdzekļu īpašnieku civiltiesiskās atbildības obligātās apdrošināšanas likums* in Latvian)
OJ	Official Journal
Property Insurance	Insurance Against Losses and Damages Within the Meaning of the Insurance Contract Act
Solvency II Directive	Directive 2009/138/EC of the European Parliament and of the Council of 25 November 2009 on the taking-up and pursuit of the business of Insurance and Reinsurance (Solvency II). Official Journal, L 335, 17.12.2009, pp. 1–155.

1. Please note that the official translation of Latvian legal acts contains the word 'Law' in their titles instead of the term 'Act'. However, the author feels that 'Act' would be more appropriate than 'Law' in translated titles of Latvian legal acts. Therefore, the former is preferred for this monograph hereinafter when referring to a particular legal act.

Preface

This monograph on insurance law in Latvia is intended to be a useful, practical and comprehensive guide for those who are interested to get familiar with regulation of insurance in Latvia, its specific approaches and related problem issues. It covers Latvian insurance law, in general, and its main institutes, covering (re)insurance supervision and insurance contract regulation. Attention is paid not only to the discussion of different insurance law matters from the perspective of Latvian insurance law in conjuncture with court practice of Latvian courts but also to problems connected with application of insurance law regulation in Latvia.

When one approaches Latvian insurance law, he or she should take into account that insurance law in Latvia is evolving regarding its regulation, related court practice and legal studies, whose number is arising especially in recent years. The fact that Latvia became a Member State of the European Union (EU) does not itself mean that EU insurance law has outlined Latvian insurance law as well. Impact of EU insurance law on insurance law regulation in Latvia is considerable; however, it is largely connected with (re)insurance supervision, and even in this area, it is neither exhaustive nor comprehensive. At the same time, insurance contract regulation is almost left to EU Member States with few exceptions such as duties of the insurer in life insurance or in the field of motor insurance. This monograph, therefore, endeavours to demonstrate the framework of Latvian (re)insurance law and its specific approaches both in general and concerning specific institutes or issues of insurance law.

Latvian insurance market is relatively small compared to the scale of the European insurance market. However, this fact alone does not mean that Latvian insurance law cannot be a potential field for interesting disputes and problems either of general character or peculiar to Latvian insurance law. The author hopes that this monograph would raise awareness of Latvian insurance law and contribute to studies in comparative law concerning insurance regulation by considering Latvian insurance law regulation as well.

Preface

General Introduction

§1. General Background Information

1. Latvia (*Latvija* [latvija] in Latvian; the official title – the Republic of Latvia (*Latvijas Republika* in Latvian)) is a country located in the northern part of Europe and is one of the three Baltic States (Lithuania and Estonia are the other two). The official state language in Latvia is Latvian. Population of Latvia is currently 2 million.[2] Latvia is a Member State of the EU since 1 May 2004 when Latvia together with the other two Baltic States (as well as certain other countries) joined the EU. Latvia is also a Member State of the World Trade Organization (WTO) since 1999 and of the Organisation for Economic Co-operation and Development (OECD) since 2016.

I. Political System

2. Political system of Latvia may be characterised as a parliamentary republic based on democratic values and the rule of law. Furthermore, Latvia is a unitary country which consists of several historical regions such as *Kurzeme* (the western part of Latvia, with Lithuania being the neighbour on the south), *Zemgale* (the central part of Latvia, again Lithuania being the neighbour on the south), *Vidzeme* (the central and eastern parts of Latvia, neighbouring Estonia on the north) and *Latgale* (the eastern part of Latvia, neighbouring Russia and Belorussia on the east and the south-east). These historical regions have no impact on Latvian political system but represent different ethnographic, historical and language dialect differences and, therefore, are traditionally distinguished. Political power is shared by the central government and municipalities on the basis of the constitutional system of Latvia.

3. Latvian constitutional system is grounded on the Constitution of the Republic of Latvia (*Latvijas Republikas Satversme* in Latvian, hereinafter Satversme).[3] The

2. Key economic data of Latvia is available in English on the web page of the Organisation for Economic Co-operation and Development (OECD). See OECD, Latvia, Selected indicators for Latvia. Available at https://data.oecd.org/latvia.htm. Alternatively, different data about Latvia is available in English on the web page of the Central Statistical Bureau – a Latvian state institution responsible for statistics. Available at http://www.csb.gov.lv/en.
3. The Constitution of the Republic of Latvia. The official translation into English is available on the official web page of the Terminology and Translation Centre at http://www.vvc.gov.lv/export/sites/default/docs/LRTA/Likumi/Constitution.doc.

Satversme was adopted on 15 February 1922 and entered into force on 7 November 1922. The Satversme was restored into force on 4 May 1990 by the Supreme Council of the Latvian Socialistic Soviet Republic. However, restoration of the force of the Satversme took place gradually until its force was fully restored on 6 July 1993.[4]

4. Article 1 of the Satversme states that 'Latvia is an independent democratic republic'. According to the principle of balance of powers of state established by the Satversme, Latvia is a parliamentary republic. The Parliament in Latvia is called *Saeima* in Latvian and is composed of one hundred representatives of the people (Article 5 of the Satversme). The Parliament enjoys broader powers than the President who is elected by the Parliament (Article 35 of the Satversme) and the Head of the Cabinet (the Prime Minister in the official text of the Satversme) who is proposed by the President (Article 56 of the Satversme) but must have a vote of confidence in the Parliament (Article 56 of the Satversme).

5. The Parliament and the people of Latvia have legislative powers (Article 64 of the Satversme), yet the Cabinet has certain legislative power within the limits set out by the Satversme. Executive power is vested with the Cabinet. The Cabinet consists of the Head of the Cabinet and Ministers (Article 55 of the Satversme). Latvian courts execute judicial power on the basis of Articles 82–86 of the Satversme. Fundamental human rights are recognised and protected by the state. The catalogue of fundamental human rights is provided by Chapter VIII (the last chapter) of the Satversme in conjuncture with international law of human rights by which Latvia is bound.

6. The Constitutional Court (*Satversmes tiesa* in Latvian) is a court of constitutional review. It adjudicates matters on the conformity of laws and other regulatory enactments in accordance with the Satversme. The Constitutional Court acts on the basis of a separate legal act called the Constitutional Court Act.[5] The Constitutional Court may annul a legal act adopted by the Parliament, the Cabinet or other institutions if this legal act is contrary to the Satversme or international treaties that bind Latvia, as well as a legal act on accession to an international treaty (signed or entered into by Latvian institutions) if its provisions do not conform with the Satversme.[6]

---

4. *See* Rodina A., Kārkliņa A. Constitutional Law and Constitutional Review, in: Tanel Kerikmäe, Kristi Joamets, Jānis Pleps, Anita Rodiņa, Tomas Berkmanas, Edita Gruodytė (eds). The Law of the Baltic States. Cham: Springer, 2017, p. 192.
5. Constitutional Court Law. The official translation into English is available on the official web page of the Terminology and Translation Centre at http://www.vvc.gov.lv/export/sites/default/docs/LRTA/Likumi/Constitutional_Court_Law.doc.
6. For the competence of the Constitutional Court, *see* Art. 16 Constitutional Court Act. For an overview of the Constitutional Court of the Republic of Latvia, *see* Rodina A., Kārkliņa A. Constitutional Law and Constitutional Review, in: Tanel Kerikmäe, Kristi Joamets, Jānis Pleps, Anita Rodiņa, Tomas Berkmanas, Edita Gruodytė (eds). The Law of the Baltic States. Cham: Springer, 2017, pp. 200–204.

The Constitutional Court has decided considerable amount of cases concerning different matters. There are two cases reviewed by the Constitutional Court which relate to private insurance matters, both of them concern motor insurance: one case[7] was related to payments of insurers into the Guarantee fund established within regulation of motor insurance,[8] but the other case concerned validity of certain provisions of a regulatory enactment of the Cabinet concerning calculation of nonmaterial damage[9] – specifically, fixed amounts of insurance redress for nonpecuniary damage caused as the result of a road traffic accident.[10] Likewise, the Constitutional Court dealt with social insurance matters in several cases, but their discussion will not be carried on as they did not fall within the area of private insurance.

II. Commerce and Industry

7. Commercial environment of Latvia is traditionally influenced by different factors such as proximity to the Baltic Sea, close ties with other Baltic States such as Lithuania and Estonia (which has also impact on the external trade discussed below and connected insurance markets among three Baltic States from the point of view of operating insurance undertakings[11]), neighbourhood relations with Russia, quality of soil, different communities and other important factors.

8. The main export market of Latvia is traditionally linked with the other EU Member States – export turnover to other EU Member States reaches almost three-fourths of Latvian total export and constitutes 72.7% of Latvian total export (in 2015)[12]. The three main exporting countries are Lithuania (19.2% of Latvian total export), Estonia (11.7%) and Russia (8.1%).[13] The three main exported goods and services are as follows: electrical machinery and equipment (13.1% of Latvian total export), machinery and mechanical appliances (6.0%) and sawn wood (5.6%).[14]

9. A similar situation also concerns Latvian import structure. The main importing countries are EU Member States whose imported goods and provided services in Latvia reach 78.7% of Latvian total import.[15] The three main importing countries are Lithuania (17.3% of Latvian total import) with Germany (11.2%) and Poland

7. Judgement of the Constitutional Court dated 9 Feb. 2004. in the Case No Nr. 2003-21-0306.
8. This fund is considered in Ch. 1, Part IX of this monograph below.
9. Judgement of the Constitutional Court dated 29 Dec. 2014. in the Case No Nr.2014-06-03.
10. The latter case is considered in Ch. 4, Part IV of this monograph below.
11. Part I, Ch. 3, §3 of this monograph below.
12. Centrālā statistikas pārvalde/Central Statistical Bureau of Latvia. Latvijas statistikas gadagrāmata 2016/Statistical Yearbook of Latvia. Riga: Centrālā statistikas pārvalde/Central Statistical Bureau of Latvia, 2017. Available at https://www.csb.gov.lv/sites/default/files/publication/2017-06/Nr%2001_Latvijas_statistikas_gadagramata_2016_Statistical%20Yearbook%20of%20Latvia_%2816_00%29_LV_EN.pdf, p. 448.
13. *Ibid.*
14. *Ibid.*, p. 449.
15. *Ibid.*, p. 448.

(11.0%) following.[16] The three main imported goods and services are: electrical machinery and equipment (12.2% of Latvian total import), machinery and mechanical appliances (9.8%) and diesel oil (6.3%).[17]

III. Financial Institutions

10. Regulation of financial system in Latvia is influenced by two factors: one – legal – factor relates to the impact of EU financial law on Latvian financial regulation. Another – economic – factor concerns the size of financial market in Latvia which is relatively small from the European point of view. Regulation of financial law is not codified in Latvia, and, consequently, subject to different legal acts, inter alia, with respect to particular financial institutions. As it is pointed out in Latvian legal literature, 'Latvian financial law regulation is represented by three groups of laws – budgetary law, tax law and financial market regulation.'[18] In this monograph, financial market regulation in relation to its participants is briefly discussed within this sub-chapter, but impact of tax law on the insurance sector will be discussed in other parts of this monograph.[19]

11. Supervision of financial market covers financial market participants such as credit institutions (banks, credit unions), insurers and reinsurers as well as insurance and reinsurance intermediaries, investment management companies, alternative investment fund managers, electronic money institutions, payment institutions, pension funds as well as financial instrument market. Each of these financial market participants and the financial instrument market are subject to a specific regulation contained in separate legal acts in conjuncture with relevant EU law. Likewise, activities with financial instruments are regulated on the basis of a special legal act called the Financial Instrument Market Act,[20] but financial securities are regulated on the basis of the Financial Security Act.[21]

12. The Financial and Capital Market Commission (*Finanšu un kapitāla tirgus komisija* in Latvian, hereinafter its abbreviation 'FKTK' in Latvian would be used) is the supervisory authority for the entire Latvian financial market. However, FKTK does not supervise all financial market participants. For instance, supervision of non-credit institutions concerning issuance of credits to consumers within the course of commercial activity is dealt by the Consumer Rights Protection Centre on the

16. *Ibid.*
17. *Ibid.*, p. 449.
18. Ketners K. Tax and Public Finance Law in Latvia, in: Tanel Kerikmäe, Kristi Joamets, Jānis Pleps, Anita Rodiņa, Tomas Berkmanas, Edita Gruodytė (eds). The Law of the Baltic States. Cham: Springer, 2017, p. 238.
19. Particularly, *see* Ch. 6, Part I and Part VIII of this monograph.
20. Financial Instrument Market Law. The official translation into English is available on the official web page of the Terminology and Translation Centre at http://vvc.gov.lv/image/catalog/dokumenti/Financial%20Instrument%20Market%20Law.docx .
21. Financial Collateral Law. The official translation into English is available on the official web page of the Terminology and Translation Centre at http://www.vvc.gov.lv/export/sites/default/docs/LRTA/Likumi/Financial_Collateral_Law.doc.

basis of Article 8 of the Consumer Rights Protection Act[22] and related regulatory enactments of the Cabinet. In addition, regulation of a consumer credit contract as a special type of loan contract is regulated separately by the above Act.[23]

13. FKTK has authority to issue binding regulations to capital market participants which are supervised by FKTK, including, on the one hand, insurers and reinsurers and, on the other hand, insurance and reinsurance intermediaries.

14. The Latvian Bank is a central bank in Latvia which was established, and operates, on the basis of a special legal act, namely Latvian Bank Act.[24] The Latvian Bank enjoys the legal status of an autonomous public law person. Its main task is to ensure stability of prices.[25]

15. Among other financial institutions which operate in Latvia one may mention a stock exchange operating in Latvian financial market which is known as *Nasdaq Baltic*; one of its exchanges is located in Riga.[26] The activity of the exchange of Nasdaq Baltic in Riga is subject to financial regulation of Latvia.

IV. Currency and Monetary Regulations

16. The national currency of Latvia was a *lat* which consisted of 100 *santims* introduced in the 1990s. After Latvia acceded to the Euro zone, euro became the official currency of Latvia. However, already since the beginning of this century, different transactions including credit (loan) contracts in Latvia employed euro as an alternative for *lat*. Euro as the official currency of Latvia was introduced on the basis of a special legal act – the Act on the Procedure for Introduction of Euro[27] (adopted on 31 January 2013, entered into force on 1 March 2013). 1 January 2014 shall be considered as the euro introduction day starting from which the two-week period for the parallel circulation of euro and *lats* was introduced.[28] The exchange rate was introduced already before that Act by the Latvian Bank for the needs of civil circulation: EUR 1 against LVL 0.702804. This exchange rate was employed for euro introduction by the above Act.

22. Consumer Rights Protection Law. The official translation into English is available on the official web page of the Terminology and Translation Centre at http://vvc.gov.lv/export/sites/default/docs/LRTA/Likumi/Consumer_Rights_Protection_Law.pdf.
23. *See* Arts 8, 8.[1], 8.[2], 12.[1] and 31 Consumer Rights Protection Act in conjuncture with a regulatory enactment of the Cabinet on consumer credit contract.
24. Latvian Bank Act. Its text in Latvian is available at https://likumi.lv/doc.php?id=65544.
25. Article 3 first sentence Latvian Bank Act.
26. For more information on Nasdaq Baltic, please visit its webpage, available at http://www.nasdaqbaltic.com/en/exchange-information/about-us/.
27. Law on the Procedure for Introduction of Euro. The official translation into English is available on the official web page of the Terminology and Translation Centre at http://vvc.gov.lv/export/sites/default/docs/LRTA/Likumi/Law_on_the_Procedure_for_Introduction_of_Euro.doc.
28. Article 7 (1) Act on the Procedure for Introduction of Euro.

17. As regards monetary regulations within civil circulation, Article 1833 of the Civil Act provides that all payments shall be made in euro (previously in *lats*). However, the note to this Article specifically envisages that specific provisions concerning calculations in foreign currency are found in the laws on credit. The Payment Services and Electronic Money Act is one of such special legal acts which concerns payment systems and electronic payments and two financial market participants, such as payment institutions and electronic money institutions, mentioned in the previous sub-chapter.

V. Insurance Business, General Organisation and Special Features

18. Insurance market of all three Baltic States, in general, and of Latvia, in particular, may be considered as relatively small if compared with the size of the EU insurance market, in general, or the largest national insurance markets within the EU, such as the German, French or Italian national insurance markets. Likewise, competition conditions within Latvian insurance market might hardly be evaluated as effective, but may rather be characterised as stable but, at the same time, as stagnant and non-developing. For instance, the amount of written insurance premiums in 2016 is almost identical to that amount in 2015.[29] The following data may be referred to characterise the size of the Latvian insurance market. The total amount of insurance premiums (*bruto*) written by Latvian insurance companies and branches of non-Member States insurers reached EUR 530 million in 2016,[30] but the world share of Latvian insurance market is relatively small and could be evaluated at approximately 0.02% of the world insurance market.

19. At the same time, general tendency in the Latvian insurance market is related to the fact that more and more insurance companies belong to foreign capital. At the moment, domestic investors own more than a half of stocks in the case of two out of five non-life insurers.[31] However, other non-life insurers and all life insurers are owned by foreign companies.

§2. Latvian Legal System and Sources of Law

20. Being a civil law country, Latvia shares the continental European civil law approach. It means that Latvian legal system is based on legal acts containing legal norms with tendency for codification of legal norms. Latvian legal system is familiar with several codifications, yet different matters and institutes are governed on the basis of specific legal acts. Likewise, Latvian legal system rejects *stare decisis* doctrine by distinguishing court practice, covering all court rulings, and settled court

29. Finanšu un kapitāla tirgus komisija [Financial and Capital Market Commission]. Pārskats par finanšu un kapitāla tirgu 2016.gadā [Overview over financial and capital market in the year of 2016]. Available in Latvian at http://www.fktk.lv/attachments/article/6203/Parskats_Q4_2016.pdf.
30. *Ibid.*
31. For factual data of Latvian insurers, *see* Part I, Ch. 3, §3 below.

practice (judicature), containing abstract legal conclusions developed by courts (usually by the Latvian Supreme Court as the highest court instance in Latvia), which are recognised as generally accepted in a particular time period.

21. Following Ancient Roman law and traditions of the continental European civil law approach, Latvian legal scholars (and this approach is echoed in legal regulation) divide law into public law and private law. Private law consists of three branches such as civil law, commercial law and private international law. The origins of the currently effective Latvian private law dates back to the regulation adopted during the Middle Ages and is influenced by different legal norms which were in force in different time periods in the current territory of Latvia.

22. Similarly, as in other jurisdictions, sharing the continental European civil law approach, Latvia pursues codification of its private law regulation; however, comprehensive codification of private (civil) law never took place in Latvia. The current regulation of private (civil) law in Latvia is based on the Latvian Civil Act (CL) which was initially adopted in 1937 and entered into force on 1 January 1938. Its force was restored in 1992–1993. This codification is largely based on the previous codification which was called the Part III of the Local Civil Laws 'Civil Law' and entered into force on 1864.

23. The understanding of sources of law in Latvia is based on the legal studies of Latvian legal scholars whose conclusions concerning sources of Latvian law are approved in court practice of Latvian courts. At the same time, this understanding arises from the whole structure of Latvian law and regulation contained by legal acts. There are distinguished permanent and additional sources of law. The former group consists of general legal principles and legal norms included in legal acts, but the latter comprises legal literature (doctrine), legislative materials and court practice.

24. The hierarchy of legal norms in Latvian law is based on Latvian legal theory approved by legal regulation and court practice of Latvian courts. In this regard, Article 15(2) of the Administrative Procedural Act[32] and Article 9(1) of the Act on Official Publications and Legal Information[33] envisage similar regulation on the hierarchy of the legal force of legal acts (the so-called external regulatory enactments) which is as follows:

(1) the Constitution (*Satversme*);
(2) laws, including Cabinet [regulatory enactments] adopted in accordance with Article 81 of the Constitution (*Satversme*);
(3) Cabinet [regulatory enactments]; and
(4) binding regulations of local governments.

32. Administrative Procedural Law. Its official translation into English is available at https://likumi.lv/ta/en/id/55567-administrative-procedure-law.
33. Law on Official Publications and Legal Information. It official translation into English is available at https://likumi.lv/ta/en/id/249322-law-on-official-publications-and-legal-information.

This hierarchy should be applied in conjuncture with sources of law. In this regard, Article 15(1) of that Act provides that:

> In administrative proceedings, institutions and courts shall apply external regulatory enactments, the legal norms of international law and the European Union (Community), as well as the general principles of law (Section 4).

Though this provision refers to administrative proceedings, the regulation undoubtedly applies to civil and criminal proceedings as well. It should be noted that this hierarchy of legal norms covers only legal norms that are included in the so-called external normative acts. Legal norms included in an internal normative act are binding only to a body which has issued this act.

In the case of a dispute over norms included in legal acts of different legal forces, precedence is given to norms of a higher force as regulated by Article 9(5) and (6) of the Act on Official Publications and Legal Information and Article 15(3)–(10) of the Administrative Procedural Act.

§3. Historical Background of Insurance and Insurance Regulation

25. After announcing independence on 18 November 1918, and its realisation, the primary task of the Latvian legislature, in the 1920s, was to establish a legal system and adoption of legal regulation, including adoption of Latvian insurance regulation.

26. Whereas insurance supervision that is to be adopted was completely new to address the needs of a newly created and relatively small country, in the case of insurance contract regulation, the situation was different. The general insurance contract regulation was included in a civil law codification known as Part III of the Local Civil Laws 'Civil Law', mentioned above, which was in force in the current territory of Latvia (except *Latgale* – a district in the eastern part of Latvia) and Estonia. This civil law codification treated insurance contract as one of the risk contracts. After the drafting and adoption of the currently effective Civil Act in 1937, and its subsequent entry into force on 1 January 1938 on the basis of a separate legal act, regulation of insurance contract was considered to be dealt with by specific legal acts but not within that civil law codification. Thus, the Latvian legislature chose to separate insurance contract regulation from other typical (i.e., subject to legal regulation) contracts regulated under law of obligations.

27. After restoration of independence of Latvia in the beginning of 1990s, insurance regulation had to be established in Latvia anew.

28. As regards insurance supervision, the insurance supervision regulation had to be established from scratch, considering the lack of insurance supervision in the Soviet Union and the legal and economic situation of that time. The first specific legal act governing insurance supervision was the Act 'On Insurance' which was adopted on 12 January 1993 and entered into force on 4 February 1993. It was later replaced by the Insurance Companies and Supervision Thereof Act on 1 September 1998 when the latter Act entered into force. The currently effective Insurance and Reinsurance Act[34] was adopted on 18 June 2015 and entered into force on 1 July 2015. The Insurance Companies and Supervision Thereof Act lost its force as from 1 January 2016. The adoption of the Insurance and Reinsurance Act was influenced by the need to implement the norms of the Solvency II Directive into Latvian law. Consequently, the Insurance and Reinsurance Act provides regulation for switching from the Solvency I supervision scheme to the Solvency II supervision scheme as introduced by the Solvency II Directive.

29. Likewise, the situation with the insurance contract was similar to that of insurance supervision. Though the force of the Civil Act was restored in 1992–1993 anew, the regulation of the Civil Act did not contain any regulation of insurance contracts as discussed above.[35] Therefore, the regulation of insurance contract also had to be established anew by considering the needs of the economic situation of that time. Regulation of insurance contract was introduced by the currently effective Latvian Insurance Contract Act (also ICA),[36] adopted on 10 June 1998 and entered into force on 1 September 1998.

30. The Insurance Contract Act was amended three times since its adoption: (1) on 1 June 2000 (in force from 1 July 2000); (2) 24 October 2002 (in force from 1 January 2003); and (3) 15 March 2007 (in force from 18 April 2007). No one portion of these amendments could be characterised as radical. These were rather fragmentary improvements or elimination of deficiencies of insurance contract regulation included in that Act. For the last time, this Act was amended on 15 March 2007 (in force from 18 April 2007) when, among other amendments, written form requirement for an insurance contract was abandoned.

31. The Cabinet approved the draft of a completely new legal act which would replace the currently effective Insurance Contract Act. This draft Act is currently being considered in the Parliament. It is not clear whether this draft Act would be ever adopted by the Parliament and, if it does, in which wording it would take place.

32. Furthermore, regulation of special insurance contracts is dealt in other legal acts. Regulation of motor insurance in Latvia has been developing separately from general insurance contract regulation included in the Insurance Contract Act discussed above. A first legal act on motor insurance was adopted in 1995 and entered into force on 1 January 1997 in the form of a regulatory enactment of the Cabinet.

---

34. Insurance and Reinsurance Act. Its text in Latvian is available at https://likumi.lv/ta/id/274969-apdrosinasanas-un-parapdrosinasanas-likums.
35. For a discussion of Latvian private law, *see* generally Linda Damane, Jānis Kārkliņš, Inese Lībiņa-Egner, Vadims Mantrovs, Daina Ose, Martins Osis, Jānis Rozenfelds, Kalvis Torgāns, Kristīne Zīle. Private Law, in: Tanel Kerikmäe, Kristi Joamets, Jānis Pleps, Anita Rodiņa, Tomas Berkmanas, Edita Gruodytė (eds.). The Law of the Baltic States. Cham: Springer, 2017, pp. 277–355.
36. Law 'On Insurance Contracts'. The official translation into English is available on the official web page of the Terminology and Translation Centre at www.vvc.gov.lv/export/sites/default/docs/LRTA /Likumi/On_Insurance_Contracts.doc.

However, this legal act was replaced by the Motor Insurance Act shortly after its entry into force, i.e., on 1 May 1997. This Motor Insurance Act was replaced by the currently effective Motor Insurance Act as of 1 May 2004. The main reason for the adoption of the currently effective Motor Insurance Act was related to the fact that Latvia joined the EU which, inter alia, implied the need to introduce regulation which would fully comply with EU motor insurance law of that time.

33. Furthermore, regulation of a marine insurance contract is subject to special legal norms, including compulsory insurance for certain marine insurance contracts, which is further discussed within compulsory insurance.[37]

34. In addition, compulsory insurance as well as regulation of specific aspects have been dealt with by separate legal acts which will be discussed in a systematic manner in Chapter 7 below.

§4. Sources of Insurance Law

I. Laws

35. Traditionally, regulation of insurance law covers two main insurance areas such as (re)insurance[38] supervision and insurance contract law. Latvia is not an exception to this traditional approach by envisaging regulation concerning both these main insurance areas. Likewise, Latvian law shares the dualistic approach for providing regulation for both these areas by regulating them separately, i.e., in separate legal acts. This dualistic approach may be explained by the development of insurance law regulation discussed above from the historical point of view and the character of regulation itself regarding both these insurance types.

36. Insurance supervision is dealt in the Insurance and Reinsurance Act. It is a legal act governing supervision of pursuing insurance and reinsurance activities and, therefore, (re)insurance supervision rules apply to insurers and reinsurers. Insurance and reinsurance intermediaries are governed by a separate legal act called Activities of Insurance and Reinsurance Intermediaries Act.[39] The legal status of the Latvian (re)insurance supervision authority – FKTK – is provided by a specific legal act, i.e., the Financial and Capital Market Commission Act, in conjunction with specific supervision rules provided by the Insurance and Reinsurance Act. In addition, supervision of both insurers and reinsurers, on the one hand, and of insurance intermediaries, on the other hand, is dealt by other laws in specific fields such as laws

37. For a discussion of compulsory insurance, *see* Ch. 7 of this Part below.
38. Hereinafter the term 're(insurance)' covers both insurance and reinsurance, but the term 'insurance' covers only insurance, i.e., excluding reinsurance.
39. Activities of Insurance and Reinsurance Intermediaries Law. The official translation into English is available on the official web page of the Terminology and Translation Centre at http://www.vvc.gov.lv/export/sites/default/docs/LRTA/Likumi/Activities_of_Insurance_and_Reinsurance_Intermediaries_Law.doc.

governing financial instruments or pension funds. Likewise, different legal acts on supervision of these subjects are adopted at the level of binding regulations of the FKTK.

37. Insurance contract law is provided by other specific legal acts. An exception is the Insurance and Reinsurance Act which provides several legal norms concerning insurance contract law.

38. Insurance contract law is subject to both general contract law and specific norms providing regulation of insurance contract law. General insurance contract law is included in a specific legal act called the Insurance Contract Act. Special legal norms are provided in other legal acts either in relation to specific insurance contracts or specific issues indirectly involving insurance contracts. As regards the former group of legal acts, one may mention the Motor Insurance Act relating to regulation of a motor insurance contract; the Maritime Code relating to fragmentary regulation of a marine insurance contract; and a set of legal norms in different legal acts imposing compulsory professional liability insurance for carrying out certain activities (such as in the case of liberal professions, security guards, builders). The latter group of legal acts relates to immigration law, requesting compulsory conclusion of travel insurance contract for visitors from third (non-EU) countries, tax law, competition and other matters.

39. As regards reinsurance contracts, they are governed by general contract law similarly as all other contracts, including insurance contracts. However, contrary to insurance contracts, legal norms of contractual nature included in the Insurance and Reinsurance Act are the ones relating to reinsurance contract regulation. As it is explicitly provided by the Insurance Contract Act, this Act does not apply to reinsurance contracts.[40]

II. Governmental Regulations

40. Separate governmental regulations in the form of *regulatory enactments* adopted by the Cabinet concern insurance contract law. Six regulatory enactments of the Cabinet are adopted in motor insurance law. Two of them concern the quantification of the amount of damage – one regarding pecuniary (material) damage caused to a person as the result of a road traffic accident and the other concerning non-pecuniary (non-material) damage caused to the person due to a road traffic accident. It should be mentioned that the latter regulatory enactment of the Cabinet was adopted by replacing the previous one after the judgment of the Constitutional Court declaring certain norms as contradicting the Satversme and, therefore, as invalid.[41]

40. Article 2(1) Insurance Contract Act.
41. *See* Part IV of this monograph below.

III. Other Legal Acts

41. The society 'Latvian Vehicles Insurers' Bureau' (*Latvijas Transportlīdzekļu apdrošinātāju birojs* in Latvian) is the Latvian national insurers' bureau in line with a national insurers' bureau in the Green Card system and EU motor insurance law.[42] Its status is regulated at the legislative level within a separate chapter of the Motor Insurance Act.[43,44] The Latvian national insurers' bureau has adopted its own regulations on different issues in respect of motor insurance such as regulation of the *bonus-malus* classes for establishing the amount of insurance premiums, calculation of damage, etc. Likewise, the FKTK has issued several binding regulations in respect of (re)insurers concerning different (re)insurance supervision matters.

IV. Private International Law

42. Private international law (PIL) issues are dealt with by EU law and separate international treaties, some of whom are binding to Latvia. If a particular issue is not regulated by these international law norms, PIL norms at the national level apply. Such national PIL norms are provided in the Introductory Part of the Latvian Civil Act and Article 2 of the Insurance Contract Act in respect of insurance contracts (as mentioned previously, reinsurance contracts are excluded from the scope of the Insurance Contract Act).

43. As regards applicable law in the case of insurance contracts, Rome I Regulation applies in addition to Rome Convention, since Latvia is bound by both these legal instruments.

44. In the case of non-contractual obligations in relation to insurance legal relationships, the Rome II Convention applies for establishing applicable law which is binding to Latvia. With respect to the application of Rome II Regulation one should mention that since 15 October 2000 Latvia is bound also by The Hague Convention of 4 May 1971 on the Law Applicable to Traffic Accidents, providing a different connecting factor than the Rome II Regulation (*lex loci delicti commissi* instead of *lex loci damni*). However, the application of this Hague Convention instead of the Rome II Regulation depends on interpretation of Article 28 of the Rome II Convention which could be resolved by the CJEU. So far, such interpretation is not provided by the CJEU.

42. Specifically, Article 1(3) Codifying Motor Insurance Directive.
43. Compulsory Civil Liability Insurance of Owners of Motor Vehicles Law. The official translation into English is available on the official web page of the Terminology and Translation Centre at http://www.vvc.gov.lv/export/sites/default/docs/LRTA/Likumi/Compulsory_Civil_Liability_Insurance.doc.
44. Chapter IV Motor Insurance Act.

V. Jurisdiction

45. Similarly as in the case with applicable law discussed above, regulation of jurisdiction is subject to EU law regulation in conjunction with international treaties forming the so-called Brussels regime. Indeed, Latvia is bound by the Brussels Convention 1968 as well as the Brussels I Regulation and the currently effective Brussels Ibis Regulation.

§5. Dispute Resolution and Arbitration

46. The Insurance Contract Act provides for special regulation on dispute resolution concerning insurance contracts (reinsurance contracts are excluded from the scope of that Act by its Article 2(1)) which is included in Article 3 ICA that governs procedures for resolution of disputes. Applicable law issues are dealt with separately in Article 2 ICA, subject to regulation of PIL at the international level discussed above.

47. Article 3(1) ICA provides that '[d]isputes related to an insurance contract shall be resolved in accordance with the procedures laid down in laws and other [..] regulations'. This provision should be understood as referring to other legal acts which contain civil procedural rules, of which Civil Procedure Act is at the centre.[45] At the same time, insurance contract parties may apply to an arbitration court. Specifically, the Insurance Contract Act allows arbitration dispute resolution by providing that by the agreement of the parties, disputes may be resolved by an arbitration court (Article 3(2) ICA). This regulation means that insurance contract parties are free to choose dispute resolution either within courts of general jurisdiction (state's courts) or through arbitration courts. An exception from this situation exists in relation to consumers as policyholders, considering that disputes with consumers shall be heard only by state's courts if an insurance contract is based on standard terms (as it usually takes place). In this situation, disputes with consumers shall be heard only by state's courts. If the arbitration clause is still included in such an insurance contract, it shall be considered as an unfair standard term on the basis of Article 6(3)(7) of the Consumer Rights Protection Act and settled court practice of Latvian courts.

48. Likewise, Article 3 ICA provides for an information duty, i.e., an insurer has to inform a policyholder if he or she is a natural person for dispute resolution in out-of-court procedures. Indeed, Article 3(3) ICA provides that prior to entering into an insurance contract an insurer has an obligation to inform a policyholder – natural person – of the existence of such procedures for the examination in an extrajudicial way of complaints and disputes which arise from the insurance contract.

45. Civil Procedure Law. The translation in English is available at https://likumi.lv/ta/en/id/50500-civil-procedure-law.

§6. CONSUMER PROTECTION

49. Consumer protection is ensured through separate legal acts on regulation of consumer protection even without the existence of any consumer protection norms in insurance law regulation itself.

50. The legal definition of the term 'consumer' is provided by the Consumer Rights Protection Act (*Patērētāju tiesību aizsardzības likums* in Latvian), and it complies with the understanding of that term within EU consumer protection law. Indeed, the consumer is a natural person who expresses a wish to purchase, or has purchased or might purchase, or use goods or a service for a purpose, which is not related to his or her economic professional activity.[46] Legal norms on protection of consumer rights may be applied if two cumulative criteria are met: both a policyholder being one of insurance contract parties (in addition to an insurer) and the person who may bring an insurance redress claim (an insured, a victim or a beneficiary depending on the insurance type by using insurance classification based on insurable object) is a consumer. However, if any of those two persons is not a consumer, consumer protection norms are not applicable in a particular dispute. However, this conclusion is not approved by the Latvian Supreme Court as far as the anonymised database of court practice of Latvian courts is concerned.

51. From the point of view of interrelation of consumer protection and insurance contracts, one may mention the following typical cases when this interrelation could take place: violation of the consumer free choice principle which is one of the violations included by the Consumer Rights Protection Act in the catalogue of consumer protection rights;[47] protection forms of consumers in insurance contracts containing standard contract terms such as unclear or imprecise contractual terms or unfair standard terms as insurance contracts are usually based on standard contract terms; regulation of financial distance contracts if an insurance contract is concluded with the assistance of distance means (such application possibility is explicitly recognised by Point 3 of the Regulatory enactment of the Cabinet on distance contract for provision of financial services[48]); and regulation of unfair commercial practices.

52. It should be noted that Latvian consumer protection law provides special legal norms concerning insurance contract relationships based on transposition of legal norms of EU law.

53. At first, in the case of unfair standard terms, the Unfair Terms Directive[49] excludes from regulation of unfair standard terms such insurance contract terms which 'clearly define or circumscribe the insured risk and the insurer's liability'

46. Article 1(3) Consumer Rights Protection Act.
47. Article 3(1) Consumer Rights Protection Act.
48. Regulations Regulatory enactment No 648 of 21 Oct. 2014 of the Cabinet ('Noteikumi par distances līgumu par finanšu pakalpojumu sniegšanu' in Latvian).
49. Council Directive 93/13/EEC of 5 Apr. 1993 on unfair terms in consumer contracts. OJ, L 95, 21.04.1993., pp. 29–34.

unless they are drafted in plain intelligible language.[50] Though this provision of the Unfair Terms Directive is not explicitly transposed into Latvian law, national regulation on standard contract terms undoubtedly should be interpreted in the light of this Directive's provision.

54. Likewise, in a distance contract for provision of financial services, the extended term of refusal right is provided if a life insurance contract being thirty days instead of the ordinary fourteen days from the date when the consumer is informed about the conclusion of a life insurance contract by distance means.[51] Likewise, one of the exceptions where a right of refusal is not permitted in the case of distance contact for provision of financial services relates to travel and luggage insurance contracts or similar short-term insurance contracts whose term is less than one month.[52] At the same time, this provision allows insurance contract parties to choose for not applying this exception.

55. In the case of aggressive commercial practices, a special regulation is provided in practices in the insurance sector. One of the cases, which are explicitly referred to in the list of aggressive commercial practises at any event, concerns requesting of documents or communication between the insurer and a consumer concerning insurance redress claim. Indeed, Article 13(4) of the Unfair Commercial Practice Prohibition Act[53] provides that a commercial practice shall be regarded as aggressive in any circumstances if an insurer as a performer of commercial practices

> requires from the consumer who wishes to submit an application regarding the receipt of insurance reimbursement according to the entered into insurance contract to submit the documents that judiciously may not be recognised as such that would justify such request, or systematically evades from the answer to the respective correspondence in order to prevent the consumer from the exercising the contractual rights.

§7. Compulsory Insurance

56. Article of 6(1) of the Insurance and Reinsurance Act envisages that insurance is voluntary, except in cases when law provides otherwise. Though this legal norm is included in regulation of insurance supervision, it covers one of the insurance contract regulation aspects as it addresses classification of insurance into voluntary and compulsory insurance.

---

50. Unfair Terms Directive, preamble, para. 15.
51. Points 19 and 20.3 of the Regulations Regulatory enactment of the Cabinet on financial distance contracts.
52. Point 21.2 Regulations Regulatory enactment of the Cabinet on financial distance contracts.
53. Unfair Commercial Practice Prohibition Law. The official translation into English is available on the official web page of the Terminology and Translation Centre at vvc.gov.lv/export/sites/default/docs/LRTA/Likumi/Unfair_Commercial_Practice_Prohibition_Law.do.doc.

57. *Compulsory insurance is envisaged* by Latvian law at least in *sixteen* cases depending on whether it relates to any of the following *three groups*: professional liability insurance; use of certain motor vehicles; and other cases. All these three groups of cases, when Latvian law requires compulsory insurance, are discussed further separately.

58. At the outset, it would be useful to point out that the Latvian legislature has chosen to replace compulsory insurance with some other types of compensation in certain cases. The case of liability of doctors is a good example for this situation. Previously, fulfilment of duties of a doctor was subject to compulsory insurance in respect of civil liability arising from damage caused during medical treatment. However, compulsory insurance in this case was later abandoned, and the Latvian legislature chose a special fund instead which is maintained by payments from medical institutions. If patients suffer damages, an appropriate compensation is provided by financial means accumulated within that fund.[54]

59. The *first group* of compulsory insurance concerns *professional liability insurance* for certain professions or activities envisaged in separate legal acts in respect of these professions or activities. Compulsory insurance is provided in the case of professions related to the court system of Latvia (sworn notary, sworn court bailiff, insolvency administrator); certain other professions such as sworn auditor, professions in the construction field, security merchant, insurance and reinsurance intermediary; or persons undertaking liability for certain activities such as manager of hydroelectrical stations or organiser of public event.

Latvian insurance law on regulation of compulsory insurance demonstrates a tendency to lay down detailed rules concerning contractual limitations in respect of insurance contracts whose compulsory conclusion is required for carrying out a respective activity. At the same time, there is little Latvian court practice available concerning disputes involving professional liability insurance in relation to compulsory insurance.

60. As regards *sworn notaries*, the Notariate Act[55] provides for compulsory insurance of civil liability for sworn notaries by providing the insurance contract conclusion duty in Article 14 and detailed rules in Chapter III of Title A. A sworn notary cannot commence fulfilling his or her duties without entering into an insurance contract for their civil liability, and the insurance contract shall be maintained in effect for the whole period of official duties of a sworn notary.[56] Sworn notaries are explicitly allowed to conclude either an individual or a group insurance contract.[57] Article 29 of the Notariate Act in conjuncture with a separate regulatory enactment of the Cabinet provides that deductibles (excess) in an insurance contract are not allowed; an insurance contract shall contain a three-year period for claim of

54. For a discussion of this fund, *see* Ch. 3, Part IX below.
55. Notariate Law. The official translation into English is available on the official web page of the Terminology and Translation Centre at http://vvc.gov.lv/export/sites/default/docs/LRTA/Likumi/Notariate_Law.doc.
56. Articles 14, 26 and 27 Notariate Act.
57. Article 24(1) Notariate Act.

insurance redress; a contract term shall not be less than one year; and a minimum liability limit (imprecisely referred to in the discussed legal acts as insurance sum) is set out in the amount of EUR 71,100 for an individual insurance contract, but EUR 711,400 – for a collective insurance contract.

61. Similar regulation as in the case of compulsory insurance for sworn notaries is envisaged in respect of *sworn court bailiffs*. Article 29 (1) and Title IV of the Bailiffs Act[58] in conjuncture with a related regulatory enactment of the Cabinet provide compulsory insurance for a sworn court bailiff. One difference between compulsory insurance regulation of sworn notary and compulsory insurance of sworn court bailiff is related to minimum liability limit. In the case of sworn court bailiff, it is provided as follows: EUR 42,600 for an individual insurance contract, but EUR 711,400 for a collective insurance contract.

62. Article 31 of the Insolvency Act[59] provides for compulsory insurance of *insolvency administrators* whose contractual issues are further specified in a separate regulatory enactment of the Cabinet. Article 31(1) of the Insolvency Act specifically provides that civil liability insurance of an insolvency administrator is perceived as a security 'for those cases when he [or she] by his [or her] activity causes losses to the state, the debtor, creditors or other persons'. These provisions of this regulatory enactment provide that the term of an insurance contract cannot be shorter than one year; the minimum liability limit shall be not less than EUR 42,600 for all administered insolvency processes; and no possibility to provide deductibles.

63. Likewise, compulsory insurance is envisaged in respect of *sworn auditors* on the basis of Article 42 of the Audit Services Act[60] and a specific regulatory enactment of the Cabinet. The minimum liability limit for a sworn auditor or a commercial company of sworn auditors shall be the total sum of income of such a sworn auditor or a company obtained in the previous reporting year from audit services (Article 42(1) and (2) of the Audit Services Act). However, the minimum liability limit shall not be less than certain sums provided by the regulatory enactment of the Cabinet, i.e. not less than EUR 42,700 for the sworn auditor but EUR 142,300 – for the commercial company of sworn auditors. An exception from this regulation of minimum liability limit shall be in the case when audit services are provided to an entity of public importance. In this case, the minimum liability amount of civil liability insurance shall be two per cent of the amount of assets of the client to be

58. Law on Bailiffs. The official translation into English is available on the official web page of the Terminology and Translation Centre at http://vvc.gov.lv/image/catalog/dokumenti/Law%20On%20Bailiffs.docx.
59. Insolvency Law. The official translation into English is available on the official web page of the Terminology and Translation Centre at http://vvc.gov.lv/image/catalog/dokumenti/Insolvency%20Law.docx.
60. Law on Audit Services. The official translation into English is available on the official web page of the Terminology and Translation Centre at http://vvc.gov.lv/image/catalog/dokumenti/On%20Audit%20Services.docx.

audited for whom such assets are the largest ones at the end of the previous reporting year, but not more than EUR 10 million (Article 42(3) of the Audit Services Act).

64. In the field of *construction*, compulsory insurance is required for pursuing two activities: one is a *construction specialist* (*būvspeciālists* in Latvian) (Article 13(10) of the Construction Act[61]), being one of the special professions in the field of construction and another is a *builder* (Article 20 of the Construction Act), irrespective of whether they build within the course of their profession or for private needs, i.e., themselves. These provisions included in the Construction Act are supplemented by a special regulatory enactment of the Cabinet providing a different kind of contractual limitations for a compulsory insurance contract in question.

65. One may establish a case when compulsory insurance is specifically provided in the insurance field and relates to *insurance intermediaries and reinsurance intermediaries*. Indeed, Article 12 of the Activities of Insurance and Reinsurance Intermediaries Act envisages compulsory insurance for pursing activities of insurance and reinsurance intermediation. Article 12(1) of this Act provides for the compulsory conclusion of a liability insurance contract for an insurance or reinsurance intermediary. Likewise, this provision defines insurable object for such a compulsory insurance contract by referring to losses ‘caused due to the professional mistakes or professional negligence of the insurance and reinsurance intermediary’.

At the same time, contrary to other cases of compulsory insurance, Article 12(1.^{1}) of the Activities of Insurance and Reinsurance Intermediaries Act provides that compulsory conclusion of an insurance contract may be alternatively replaced by a bank guarantee in the amount corresponding to a minimum liability limit discussed below.

Article 12 of the Activities of Insurance and Reinsurance Intermediaries Act envisages different kinds of contractual limitations for a compulsory insurance contract in question. Among these limitations one may mention the territorial coverage that shall be the territory of the EU; minimum annual liability limit in the amount of EUR 1,680,300, but for a single insurance event, not less than EUR 1,120,200; deductibles may be envisaged in the amount of EUR 10,000; extended term for submitting claims which cannot be shorter than three years since expiry of the contract term.

66. Professional patent attorneys are subject to compulsory conclusion of a liability insurance contract for damages caused by their professional activity. This duty was envisaged for the first time when the Industrial Property Institutions and Procedures Act[62] entered into force on 1 January 2016. Article 130(2) of this Act

61. Construction Law. The official translation into English is available on the official web page of the Terminology and Translation Centre at http://vvc.gov.lv/export/sites/default/docs/LRTA/Likumi/Construction_Law.doc.

62. Law on Industrial Property Institutions and Procedures. The official translation into English is available on the official web page of the Terminology and Translation Centre at http://vvc.gov.lv/image/catalog/dokumenti/Law%20on%20Industrial%20Property%20Institutions%20and%20Procedures.docx.

specifically envisages the duty of a professional patent attorney to conclude a liability insurance contract before the commencement of his or her professional activity, and to ensure validity of the insurance agreement constantly throughout the time of his or her professional activity.

Article 130(3) of the above Act provides that a minimum liability limit shall be 100 minimum monthly wages (the minimum monthly wage in Latvia is established in the amount of EUR 430 since 1 January 2018) in the case of an individual insurance agreement, but in the case of a group insurance contract – 200 minimum monthly wages.

Compulsory insurance regulation provided by Article 130 of the above Act is supplemented with a provision which is not envisaged in other compulsory insurance cases and which refers to the limitation of liability of professional patent attorneys for damage they made by their professional activity within a liability limit. Specifically, Article 130(4) of the Industrial Property Institutions and Procedures Act provides such regulation which, considering its importance, is quoted in full:

> In case of setting in of the circumstances referred to in Paragraph one of this Section [i.e. damage caused by a professional patent attorney within its professional activity – author's remark], the liability of the professional patent attorney shall be limited to the amount of insurance of civil liability, determined in the insurance agreement, and it shall not be less than that laid down in Paragraph three of this Section [i.e. within liability limit discussed above – author's remark].

As one may notice, this provision refers not so much to compulsory insurance, but to civil liability in the specific case, i.e., civil liability of professional patent attorneys. Considering such a rare regulation has been included in this provision, it remains to be seen its interpretation by Latvian courts. As far as the anonymised database of court practice of Latvian courts is concerned, there is no one case decided by Latvian courts involving application of this provision.

67. Compulsory insurance is also provided for *security merchants* on the basis of Article 25 of the Security Activity Act and a related regulatory enactment of the Cabinet which provides contractual limitations for a compulsory insurance contract in question. For instance, this regulatory enactment provides that minimum liability limit shall be at least 10% of the annual turnover of a particular security merchant but not less than EUR 142,200 per year.

68. Compulsory insurance is provided for *managers of hydroelectrical stations* on the basis of Article 4(7) and (8) of the Act 'On Safety of Hydrotechnical Buildings of Hydroelectrical Stations' and a related regulatory enactment of the Cabinet which provides contractual limitations for a compulsory insurance contract in question.

69. Similarly, compulsory insurance is provided in respect of *organisers of public event* in accordance with the Act on Safety of Public Entertainment and Festivity

Events[63]. Specifically, compulsory civil liability insurance is provided for the organiser of a public event by Articles 7(6) and 10(2)(8) of that Act. This Act as well as a specific regulatory enactment of the Cabinet provide minimum liability limit for insurance of civil liability of organisers of public event. The amount of minimum liability limit for one public event depends on the planned number of attendees of the event: if the number of attendees could be estimated as not more than 100, the minimum liability limit is set in the amount of EUR 2,845; from 101–1,000 – EUR 10,670; more than 1,000 – EUR 14,230. An exception is provided if it is intended to use sources of increased danger or pyrotechnics during the event – in this case the amount of minimum liability limit as mentioned above shall be doubled.

70. *Sworn attorneys* are placed in interesting situation concerning compulsory insurance. In their case, compulsory insurance is not currently provided by Latvian law. However, if a sworn attorney has not insured his or her professional civil liability, the sworn attorney shall inform a client about the fact of non-insurance (Article 114 of the Advocacy Act of the Republic of Latvia).

71. Another type of cases of compulsory insurance covers certain types of motor vehicles travelling on roads, in the sea or in the air. Rules requiring compulsory insurance for such vehicles are provided separately in different legal acts.

72. Compulsory insurance is required for the use of *land motor vehicles travelling on roads* covered by the concept of motor insurance. Compulsory insurance in relation to insurance of civil liability of motor vehicle drivers in respect of the use of motor vehicles in road traffic is governed by a special act – the Motor Insurance Act (in conjuncture with EU motor insurance law) discussed in Part IV below. Contrary to professional liability insurance discussed above, there are extensive court practice concerning motor insurance which is also discussed in Part IV below.

73. Likewise, compulsory insurance is provided for civil liability in relation to the use of motor vehicles operating in *the sea* such as ships of certain sizes. Marine insurance in Latvia is regulated by the Maritime Code,[64] especially its Chapter XII^1 on insurance of a ship in respect of maritime claims.

74. Article 56^1(2) of the Maritime Code provides the legal definition of the concept 'insurance' within the meaning of that chapter by envisaging that

> insurance is insurance whether it is self-insurance, with or without a deductible, as well as other similar financial security.

63. Law on Safety of Public Entertainment and Festivity Events. The official translation into English is available on the official web page of the Terminology and Translation Centre at http://vvc.gov.lv/image/catalog/dokumenti/Law_on_Safety_of_Public_Entertainment_and_Festivity_Events.doc.
64. Maritime Code. The official translation into English is available on the official web page of the Terminology and Translation Centre at http://vvc.gov.lv/export/sites/default/docs/LRTA/Likumi/Maritime_Code.doc

75. It should be taken into account that neither this nor any other provision in the Maritime Code specifies the term 'financial security' except the requirement that the insurance within the meaning of this chapter should be proved by a respective document (Article $56.^1(3)$ of the Maritime Code). Article $56.^1(1)$ of the Maritime Code envisages compulsory insurance in respect of Latvian ships which have certain tonnage, i.e., if tonnage of a Latvian ship is 300 tonnage units or more, the shipowner, bareboat charterer or other person responsible for the operation of the ship has a duty to insure the ship for maritime claims. In this situation, requirements for insurance sum are provided by Article $56.^2$ of the Maritime Code in conjuncture with Articles 69 (1)–(2) and 70(1) of that Code.

76. Compulsory insurance is provided also in relation to the use of *aircrafts* and other civil aviation objects and equipment by a special legal act – the Aviation Act.[65] Article 111 of the Aviation Act is the central to this regulation. Article 111(1) of that Act provides that this duty is provided upon owners or air operators of such aircrafts. Likewise, this provision provides different insurance objects of such insurance contract, namely: an aircraft and other civil aviation objects and equipment; members of a flight crew; civil liability insurance both for damage caused to passengers or cargo and damage caused to third persons by an aircraft in flight or any objects separated therefrom.

Article 111(2)–(4) of the Aviation Act provides additional rules when compulsory insurance is required as in the case of training for the use of an aircraft; certain non-members of a flight crew; and for persons who are engaged in aviation as a sport.

In addition, compulsory insurance of civil liability for damage caused to third parties and environment is also required from owners of unmanned aircrafts if their total landing weight exceeds 1.5 kilograms.[66]

77. Finally, there are *other cases* not falling within any of the above two groups when the Latvian legislature chose compulsory insurance, for instance, certain types of *voluntary work* on the basis of the Voluntary Work Act and a related regulatory enactment of the Cabinet.

78. In addition, Latvian insurance supervision law provides specific regulation concerning conclusion of a compulsory insurance contract. Article 192^2 of the Insurance and Reinsurance Act provides that compulsory insurance contracts shall contain insurance contract provisions which arise from legal acts that envisage compulsory insurance. But if a compulsory insurance contract does not comply with the requirements envisaged by a legal act requiring compulsory insurance, it is

65. Law 'On Aviation'. The official translation into English is available on the official web page of the Terminology and Translation Centre at http://www.vvc.gov.lv/export/sites/default/docs/LRTA/Likumi/On_Aviation.doc.
66. Point 9 of the Regulatory enactment of the Cabinet No 737 'Procedure for the conduct of unmanned aircrafts and other types of aerial vehicles which do not qualify as an aircraft' dated 22 Nov. 2016.

assumed that such a contract is not concluded. Latvian insurance practice demonstrates that there could be such a situation when an insurer offers the insurance contract provisions in respect of compulsory insurance, especially concerning professional civil liability insurance, which do not correspond to mandatory rules provided by Latvian legal acts discussed previously. However, as far as the anonymised database of court practice of Latvian courts is concerned, it is not possible to establish any court case where Latvian courts have addressed this problem issue.

Part I. The Insurance Company

Chapter 1. The Insurance Company: Its Form

§1. Public or Private Nature

79. The Solvency II Directive allows broad discretion for EU Member States in choosing a respective legal form for insurance undertakings.[67] The exhaustive list of legal forms to be used for insurance undertakings is available in the Annex III to the Solvency II Directive.

80. Latvia has chosen three different types of legal forms which could be employed by insurance undertakings, and these are included in the Annex III to the Solvency II Directive. As regards Latvian national insurance supervision law, these legal forms are included in the legal definition of the term 'insurance company' and are as follows: joint stock company (JSC), European Commercial Company (i.e., SE, *European societas*) and mutual insurance cooperative society.[68] All these legal forms are of private nature and refer to legal persons of private law.[69] As a result, the term 'insurer' as referred to in Latvian insurance law, particularly, in the Insurance Contract Act, is not defined (contrary to the term 'policyholder'[70]) but understood as covering an insurance undertaking established in Latvia which took one of these legal forms and obtained a prior authorisation (i.e., a licence).

81. Currently, Latvian law deals with insurance undertakings established on the basis of private law which are covered by the term 'legal persons of private law'. Therefore, Latvian law, as it stands now, does not envisage an insurance institution of public nature that would be entitled to pursue (re)insurance activity. This explains why none of the Latvian insurance undertaking enjoys an individual exemption under the Solvency II Directive (specifically, its Articles 8 and 10).

67. Article 17 (1) Solvency II Directive.
68. Article 1 (5) Supervision Insurance and Reinsurance Act.
69. For a discussion of Latvian commercial law and its subjects, *see* generally Kārkliņš J., Mantrov V. Company Law and Insolvency Law, in: Tanel Kerikmäe, Kristi Joamets, Jānis Pleps, Anita Rodiņa, Tomas Berkmanas, Edita Gruodytė (eds). The Law of the Baltic States. Cham: Springer, 2017, pp. 304–320.
70. Its legal definition is provided by Art. 1(6) ICA.

§2. FACTUAL DATA

82. As of March 2018, there were six insurance undertakings in Latvia as Latvian insurance companies: four of them were non-life insurance companies, and two were life insurance companies.[71] The number of insurance companies in Latvia in the past years did not exceed ten, and usually there were more non-life insurance companies than life insurance companies. In addition, other EU insurers operate in Latvia based on the Single European licence, making use either of the freedom of establishment or of the freedom to provide services. As regards freedom of establishment, as of March 2018, there were eleven EU insurers that carry out insurance activity through branches. These EU insurers come from two other Baltic States and Sweden.[72] As regards freedom to provide services, there were more than five hundred EU insurers as of March 2018, which may carry out insurance activities in Latvia by employing that freedom.[73]

71. FKTK. Licences granted to insurance companies. Available in Latvian at http://www.fktk.lv/lv/tirgus-dalibnieki/apdrosinasana/apdrosinasanas-sabiedribam-pie.html.
72. FKTK. Freedom of establishment. Available in Latvian at http://www.fktk.lv/lv/tirgus-dalibnieki/apdrosinasana/pakalpojumu-sniedzeji-no-eez/dibinasanas-briviba.html.
73. FKTK. Freedom to provide services. Available in Latvian at http://www.fktk.lv/lv/tirgus-dalibnieki/apdrosinasana/pakalpojumu-sniedzeji-no-eez/pakalpojumu-sniegsanas-briviba.htm.l.

Chapter 2. Access to Business: Authorisation – Requirements and Procedures

83. Insurance or reinsurance activity may be pursued by an insurance or reinsurance company in Latvia only after obtaining a prior authorisation. The legal basis for obtaining the prior authorisation at the EU law level is currently provided by the Solvency II Directive whose norms in Latvia are transposed into the Insurance and Reinsurance Act.

84. Obtaining a prior authorisation in the form of a licence is dealt with separately for insurance and reinsurance respectively in Chapters III and IV of the Insurance and Reinsurance Act. Common rules for insurance and reinsurance for obtaining the licence are included in Chapter V of the said Act. Furthermore, the regulation of announcement procedure for insurers from other EU Member States using either freedom of establishment or freedom to provide services is dealt with in Chapters XVIII–XX of the Insurance and Reinsurance Act. In addition, the procedure for obtaining a prior authorisation in the form of a licence for a branch of a non-EU Member State insurer is dealt separately in Chapter XXI of this Act.

85. As regards insurance, a prior authorisation, i.e., a licence, shall be obtained for each class of either non-life or life insurance separately. These classes are listed in Article 19 of the Insurance and Reinsurance Act. Separation of life and non-life insurance is ensured in such a way that life insurers may act within personal insurance area, but non-life insurers could act in all insurance types except life insurance and associated areas with life insurance, such as pensions insurance.[74]

86. In order to obtain a licence, a company shall satisfy certain requirements set out in Article 21 of the Insurance and Reinsurance Act, such as one of the prescribed legal forms characterised above; fulfilment of solvency and financial requirements; establishment of a management system; and submission of necessary documents. Documents to be submitted and requirements towards them are regulated in Articles 22–23 of the Insurance and Reinsurance Act.

87. A similar procedure is provided for obtaining a licence in the case of reinsurance activities, yet subject to specific provisions, such as types of reinsurance where a prior authorisation should be obtained; non-prohibition to carry out simultaneously insurance and reinsurance activity; requirements and documents different from those provided in the case of obtaining the licence for pursuing an insurance activity.

74. For an overview of life insurance and associated areas with life insurance, *see* Chs 3–4, Part V below.

88. Common provisions relating to insurance and reinsurance companies are provided in Chapter V of the Insurance and Reinsurance Act, including requirements as to who may be a stockholder or a shareholder of such a company and the list of exhaustive grounds for refusal of the licence.

89. Similarly, stricter procedures than in the case of a domestic insurance company discussed above are provided separately in the case of a branch of a non-Member State insurer by the Insurance and Reinsurance Act as mentioned previously.

Chapter 3. Supervision

90. Supervision rules of insurance companies (as well as reinsurance companies) are envisaged in Latvian law within the framework of Solvency II as introduced by the Solvency II Directive and related legal acts adopted by EU institutions. Yet, the Latvian legislature provided certain rules for situations when the Solvency II Directive allowed for a discretion for an EU Member State.

§1. Solvency Control

91. The legal regime of solvency control of insurance and reinsurance companies is provided by the Insurance and Reinsurance Act within the supervision framework provided by the Solvency II Directive. The Insurance and Reinsurance Act exploits the concept of own capital to ensure financial stability of insurance and reinsurance companies.

Own capital consists of the usable own capital in the amount of solvency capital requirement and the usable basic own capital in the amount of minimum capital requirement.[75] Chapter XIV Insurance and Reinsurance Act contains detailed rules on calculation of a solvency capital requirement and a minimum capital requirement.

Generally, the solvency capital requirement is calculated on the basis of either a standard formula or an internal model in full or in part.[76] At the same time, the minimum capital requirement is calculated by using the absolute minimum value.[77] The solvency capital requirement is more based on an individualistic model depending on the specifics of a particular insurance undertaking, but the minimum capital requirement is more collective, which is based on the predefined absolute minimum value, yet in consideration with the solvency capital requirement.[78]

Specifically, Article 130(3) of the Insurance and Reinsurance Act envisages the absolute minimum value of the minimum capital requirement which is as follows:

(1) non-life insurance companies, including captive insurance companies, which perform insurance according to the non-life insurance types referred to in Article 19, paragraph 1, Points 10, 11, 12, 13, 14 and 15, shall have EUR 3.7 million, but other non-life insurance companies, EUR 2.5 million;
(2) life insurance companies, including captive insurance companies, which have obtained the licence in life insurance, shall have EUR 3.7 million;
(3) reinsurance companies shall have EUR 3.6 million, but captive reinsurance companies, EUR 1.2 million;
(4) insurance companies, which simultaneously perform non-life insurance and life insurance, shall have the sum of absolute minimum values of the minimum capital requirement referred to in Points 1 and 2 above.

75. Articles 116 and 117 Insurance and Reinsurance Act.
76. Article 119(1) Insurance and Reinsurance Act.
77. Article 130(2) Insurance and Reinsurance Act.
78. *See* Art. 130(2) Insurance and Reinsurance Act.

An absolute minimum value shall be calculated by each insurance undertaking every three months and submitted to the FKTK.[79] The absolute minimum value as referred to above is subject to review once in five years and indexed in accordance with the inflation rate.[80]

§2. Supervision of Tariffs and Insurance Conditions

92. Supervision of insurance contract terms and amounts of insurance premiums is not currently envisaged in a direct form. Previously, it was provided by a special legal act adopted in the form of regulations adopted by the FKTK. However, the last such specific legal act lost its force as of 29 April 2003 due to non-compliance with EU (then European Community (EC)) insurance law.

93. Therefore, since Latvian insurance law was brought in line with EU insurance law, supervision of insurance contract terms and amounts of insurance premiums was abandoned. As regards EU law, since the entry into force of the third generation of non-life and life insurance directives such a supervision issue was explicitly disallowed, and currently this rule is maintained by the Solvency II Directive.[81] At the same time, supervision of insurance contract terms is provided in an indirect way, such as through consumer protection law and restrictions or limitations concerning certain insurance contract terms.

79. Article 130(4) Insurance and Reinsurance Act.
80. Article 130(5) Insurance and Reinsurance Act.
81. Articles 154 and 181 of the Solvency II Directive.

Chapter 4. Technical Reserves and Investments

94. Technical reserves are one of the instruments to control solvency and the amount of obligations with respect to insurance and reinsurance companies. The legal definition of technical reserves (or technical provisions in the meaning of EU insurance supervision regulation[82]) is provided by the Insurance and Reinsurance Act, which provides that technical reserves consist of the sum of a best estimate and a risk margin.[83] Regulation of technical reserves is further provided by Chapter XIII of the Insurance and Reinsurance Act by transposing corresponding norms of the Solvency II Directive.[84] Regulation of technical reserves is closely linked with valuation of assets and obligations regulated under Article 98 of the Insurance and Reinsurance Act.[85]

95. Regulation of investments of assets of insurance and reinsurance companies is dealt separately by technical reserves. This regulation is drafted by closely following regulation of this issue under EU insurance law. Specifically, Chapter XVI (Articles 131–138) of the Insurance and Reinsurance Act[86] introduces the so-called prudent person principle for investments of assets and envisages the principle of freedom of investment as provided by the Solvency II Directive. Specifically, Article 132(1) of the Insurance and Reinsurance Act regulates the former principle by explicitly mentioning it in Article 131 of that Act and providing that insurance and reinsurance companies shall invest their assets only in such assets and financial instruments that could be duly evaluated (Article 132(1) of the Insurance and Reinsurance Act).[87] At the same time, the first sentence of Article 132(2) of the Insurance and Reinsurance Act goes on with the latter principle by envisaging that insurance and reinsurance companies shall draft and approve their investment policy and procedure.

82. Articles 76 et seq Solvency II Directive.
83. Article 1(45) Insurance and Reinsurance Act (corresponds to Art. 77 (1) Solvency II Directive).
84. Articles 76 et seq Solvency II Directive.
85. Article 75 Solvency II Directive concerning valuation assets and liabilities.
86. Articles 132–135 Solvency II Directive.
87. Article 132(1) the Insurance and Reinsurance Act.

Chapter 5. Accountancy

96. Accountancy of the insurance company is subject to general regulation of accounting with the exception of certain specific provisions that are provided by insurance supervision rules. These specific provisions are included in Chapter XI (Articles 86–91) of the Insurance and Reinsurance Act concerning accounting, annual report, revision and publicity of information. Such a division of general and specific rules is provided by this Act itself, by envisaging that an insurance and reinsurance company, or a non-EU Member State insurer's branch, carries out accounting according to the Act 'On accounting' and this Act.[88] Likewise, additional rules for accounting and drafting annual reports are provided by regulations issued by the FKTK.

97. Article 87 of the Insurance and Reinsurance Act concerns terms for drafting annual reports of insurance and reinsurance companies and submitting to competent state institutions (State Revenue Service which is the state institution responsible for administration of taxes and the Enterprise Register which is an administrative institution responsible for the maintenance of the commercial register). Likewise, Article 88 of the Insurance and Reinsurance Act provides the duty of disclosure of an annual report together with the report of a sworn auditor either in the web page of a particular insurance or reinsurance company or in another manner. This duty is accompanied by another duty to disclose annually a report for its solvency and financial standing as provided by Article 91 ICA.

98. Specific rules are provided in Articles 89–90 of the Insurance and Reinsurance Act in respect of a sworn auditor who shall draft a report concerning an annual report, including his or her duty to inform the FKTK immediately if important shortcomings in the activity of an insurance company or reinsurance company are established (Article 90 ICA).

88. Article 86(1) ICA.

Chapter 6. Taxation of the Company

99. Taxation of the insurance company is subject to general regulation of tax law,[89] specifically enterprise income tax. Regulation of enterprise income tax contains specific provisions in relation to insurance and reinsurance companies which are further discussed in Part VIII below.

89. For an overview of Latvian tax law, *see* generally Ketners K. Tax and Public Finance Law in Latvia, in: Tanel Kerikmäe, Kristi Joamets, Jānis Pleps, Anita Rodiņa, Tomas Berkmanas, Edita Gruodytė (eds). The Law of the Baltic States. Cham: Springer, 2017, pp. 238–248.

Part II. The Insurance Contract: General

Chapter 1. Generalities (Characteristics, Interpretation, Categories, General Principles)

100. Latvian insurance contract law could be characterised as evolving, both as regards the development of the regulation and the understanding of insurance contract principles and their regulation. Latvian general regulation of insurance contract, as it stands now, could be considered as employing old-fashioned approaches rather than modern approaches: for instance, the approach for reporting of material facts to an insurer by a policyholder before conclusion of an insurance contract; the length of limitation term; restricted immunity in recourse claim regulation; and others which are discussed within this part of the monograph.

101. Latvian insurance contract law is essentially grounded on legal regulation as Latvian courts have not independently developed general principles of insurance contract law, and as they are inclined to strictly stick to the wording of the legal rules. At the same time, the approach of Latvian courts, at least in recent years, is more and more becoming sophisticated and evaluated by their searching for the balance between interests of insurance contract parties and persons who may claim insurance redress from the insurer.

102. Latvian courts deal with different kinds of insurance contract disputes in their daily practices, reflecting the extent of Latvian insurance market. As far as the author of these lines is aware, there are no public data available for court cases reviewed by Latvian courts involving insurance contract matters. However, as it could be concluded from the anonymised database of court practice of Latvian courts, the Latvian Supreme Court (a cassation instance in the Latvian court system[90]) reviews approximately ten court cases each year involving insurance contract issues, mainly motor insurance cases. At the same time, one may conclude on the basis of court practices, so far Latvian courts have avoided establishing and,

90. On a brief discussion of Latvian court system, *see* Rodina A., Kārkliņa A. Constitutional Law and Constitutional Review, in: Tanel Kerikmäe, Kristi Joamets, Jānis Pleps, Anita Rodiņa, Tomas Berkmanas, Edita Gruodytė (eds). The Law of the Baltic States. Cham: Springer, 2017, p. 200.

consequently, maintaining their own developed approaches on application of insurance contract law. An exception from this situation could be the principle of indemnity (it is referred to as the principle of compensation in the terminology of Latvian insurance contract law) whose understanding is based on settled court practice of Latvian courts.[91]

103. General principles of Latvian insurance contract law may be considered as follows: no insurance without insurable risk, no insurance without insurable interest, the indemnity principle (which is covered in Latvia by the term 'compensation principle' (*kompensācijas princips* in Latvian)) as well as the utmost good faith (*uberrima fidei* in Latin) principle in reporting of material facts.[92] In addition, general civil law principles, such as good faith principle, are also applicable, although they have not been applied in insurance contract disputes by Latvian courts *expressis verbis* so far (as far as the anonymised database of court practice of Latvian courts is concerned).

104. In Latvian court practice, the most attention was paid to the indemnity principle which was applied in a number of judgments by Latvian courts, including the Latvian Supreme Court. Specifically, according to settled court practice of Latvian courts, the indemnity principle precludes an insured (a victim, a beneficiary) to make profit out of the occurrence of the insured risk (i.e., the insured event).

91. For a review of this principle, *see* Ch. 1, Part III below.
92. These principles are discussed in Latvian legal literature (*see* Rone D. Apdrošināšanas tiesību principu ietekme uz apdrošināšanas atlīdzības izmaksu. Available in Latvian at https://www.dukonference.lv/files/proceedings_of_conf/53konf/tiesibas/Rone.pdf).

Chapter 2. Essential Elements (*Essentialia Negotii*) of an Insurance Contract

105. Establishing of essential elements of a contract is one of the prerequisites for the contract to enter into force. The Insurance Contract Act provides regulation for essential elements of an insurance contract which are included in the legal definition of the term 'insurance contract'. This legal definition is included in Article 1(5) ICA which provides as follows:

> [A]greement between an insurer and policyholder by which the policyholder undertakes a duty to pay insurance premiums in the manner, time periods and amount specified in the contract, as well as to meet other duties specified in the contract, and the insurer undertakes a duty to pay out the insurance compensation to the person indicated in the contract upon the occurrence of the insurable event.

106. *Five essential elements* may be deduced from this legal definition each of which is defined separately in Article 1 ICA, i.e., insurable object, insurable risk, insurable interest, insurance sum and insurance premium. At the same time, Latvian legal scholars have justly noticed discrepancy between this provision and Article 7(1) ICA[93] as the latter refers to other provisions that shall be mandatorily included in an insurance policy, i.e., Articles 6(2) and 55 ICA, that contain the list of different elements of an insurance contract which shall be agreed upon for the contract to enter into force as indicated in Article 7(1) ICA. This discrepancy may be explained by the fact that the initial wording of the Insurance Contract Act envisaged a written form requirement for an insurance contract. However, when the written form requirement in the case of the insurance contract was abandoned in 2007, Articles 6(2) and 55 ICA were not amended accordingly. Therefore, this discrepancy should be interpreted in favour of five essential elements of an insurance contract as envisaged by the legal definition of the term 'insurance contract' by Article 1(5) ICA. A similar opinion is expressed in Latvian legal literature by pointing out that not all insurance contract elements listed in Article 6(2) ICA (and obviously also in Article 55 ICA) may be considered as essential elements of an insurance contract.[94]

107. Insurable risk is defined separately in Article 1(13) ICA as 'insurance risk' in the following wording:

> [A]n event provided for by the insurance contract, independent of the will of an insured person, the occurrence of which is possible in the future.

As one may notice from this legal definition of an insurable risk, it encompasses two essential and generally accepted elements of insurable risk, i.e., uncertainty and

93. Torgāns K. Saistību tiesības: mācību grāmata. R.: TNA, 2014, 447.lpp.
94. *Ibid.*

contingency. If insurable risk does not appear at the moment of entry into force of the insurance contract or has disappeared at the time of occurrence of an insured risk, such insurance contract is not valid. This conclusion reflects one of insurance contract law principles which provides that there is no insurance without insurable risk.

108. The principle characterised above as no insurance without insurable risk is laid down in Article 11 ICA. Article 11(1) ICA provides that

> If at the time when an insurance contract comes into force the probability of occurrence of insurance risk does not exist or the insurance risk has already occurred, the insurance contract shall not be in force from the moment of entering into thereof.

109. Depending on the knowledge of a policyholder, other paragraphs of Article 11 ICA provide for regulation for repayment of insurance premium.

110. A similar regulation structure exists also with respect to an insurable interest as another essential element of an insurance contract. The legal definition of the term 'insurable interest' is provided by Article 1(2) ICA which envisages that insurable interest is 'interest not to suffer damages upon the occurrence of insurance risk'. As it could be seen from this legal definition, the term 'damages' is not precise as this term excludes non-pecuniary damage. Hence, the term 'damages' in this legal definition could rather be replaced by the term 'harm' considering insurable object in personal insurance. Article 10 ICA deals with lack of insurable interest. Article 10(1) ICA encapsulates the principle discussed above that no insurance is possible without insurable interest:

> If at the time of an insurance contract entering into force, the insurable interest does not exist, the insurance contract shall not be in force from the moment of entering into thereof.

111. Further paragraphs of Article 10 ICA provide consequences of that lack in relation to repayment of insurance premium depending on the knowledge of a policyholder.

112. The Latvian Supreme Court has dealt more with the term of insurable interest than with the term of insurable risk so far. For instance, in one of its cases, the Latvian Supreme Court reviewed the situation when a co-owner owning one-third of the living house insured the house against fire risk in the full amount. As the insurer provided insurance redress in the amount of one-third of the insured sum, the insured co-owner claimed insurance redress in the full amount in the court. By sustaining the judgment of the appeal instance court, which approved the correctness of the insurer's decision, the Latvian Supreme Court indicated that the insured co-owner could claim not more than the amount of losses that were suffered as a result of the occurrence of the insured risk, i.e., on the basis of the indemnity principle.[95]

113. It should be noted that neither in this nor in other cases Latvian courts did not clearly distinguish the indemnity principle from the concept of insurable interest. In the court case discussed, the correct reasoning would be if the court would refer to the requirement of insurable interest than the indemnity principle instead.

114. Another shortcoming of this case relates to the fact that it remains unclear whether another co-owner may claim insurance redress for his or her respective co-owned share of the living house. If insurance of the living house could be recognised as insurance for the benefit of third parties which is possible under Latvian insurance contract law as discussed below,[96] such claim should be considered as well grounded.

115. Another case was reviewed by the Latvian Supreme Court on the grounds of the law and involved insurable interest related to insurance of a living house. Latvian courts, including the Latvian Supreme Court, dealt with the issue whether insurance redress should be provided to the person who was the owner of the insured object (in this case – a living house) at the moment of the occurrence of the insured risk: the owner should be established either on the basis of records entered into the Land Register or the person who regained property rights for that house but was not registered as the owner yet. In this situation, the Latvian Supreme Court gave priority to the person who is recognised as the owner of an immovable property on the basis of records entered in the Land Register.[97] Though Latvian courts decided this case on the basis of the principle of indemnity, it could be clearly seen from the facts that this case related to establishing insurable interest.

---

95. Judgment of the Latvian Supreme Court of the Republic of Latvia dated 13 Mar. 2013 in Case No SKC-145/2013.
96. *See* Ch. 7 of this Part.
97. Judgment of the Latvian Supreme Court of the Republic of Latvia dated 30 Oct. 2002 in Case No SKC-469, in: Jurista vārds, 2003.gada 21.janvāris, Nr. 3.

Chapter 3. Formation of the Insurance Contract (Pre-contractual Phase, Actual Formation of the Contract, Validity Requirements, Proof of the Contract; Insurance Policies)

116. The Insurance Contract Act sufficiently regulates formation of an insurance contract. Indeed, Article 5 ICA provides that a policyholder must report information which is requested by the insurer in the insurance proposal. As it is justly stated in Latvian legal literature, an insurance proposal cannot be considered as a contract offer.[98] Afterwards, the insurer proceeds with the draft insurance contract which could be considered as a contract offer.

117. The policyholder *expresses its acceptance* in the manner prescribed by the Insurance Contract Act. Article 7(2) ICA is a leading norm for regulation of this issue, which would be useful to quote in full:

> [A] policyholder shall express his or her consent to the entering into an insurance contract in accordance with the offer of the insurer by paying the insurance premium in the manner, time period and amount determined in the offer of the insurer, or also express his or her consent in another way determined in the offer of the insurer. In case of a dispute the insurer has a duty to prove the fact of entering or not entering into an insurance contract.

The policyholder may express acceptance either by payment of insurance premium or in any other way as indicated by the insurance contract as both possibilities are explicitly admitted in the first sentence of the quote.

Likewise, as one may notice from this quote, the second sentence of Article 7(2) ICA puts the burden of proof for validity of the insurance contract on the shoulders of the insurer solely. This conclusion does not mean that a policyholder may not object to or – on the contrary – insist on the validity of the insurance contract; however, he or she must prove his or her allegations in this situation.

118. Formation of an insurance contract discussed above is regulated by the Latvian Insurance *separately from entry into force* of the insurance contract through Article $7.^2$ ICA.

Regulation included in Article $7.^2$ ICA is based on the idea that an insurance contract is a real contract whose entry into force is established by the payment of an insurance premium (*re contrahitur obligatio*). Article $7.^2(1)$ ICA provides that:

> If parties agree that an insurance premium or its first part is paid after entry into effect of an insurance contract, the insurance contract shall enter into effect with the date determined in the insurance contract after payment of the insurance premium or its first part within the time period determined in the insurance contract. If the insurance premium or its first part is not paid until the time

98. Torgāns K. Saistību tiesības: mācību grāmata. R.: TNA, 2014, 447.lpp.

> period determined in the insurance contract, the insurance contract shall be considered as not valid in conformity with the provisions of Paragraphs two, three and four of this Section.

The first sentence of the quote deals with the situation when the insurance premium is not paid fully, within the term, when the insurance contract is entered into force. In case if insurance premium or its first instalment is paid within the term envisaged in the contract, this contract enters into force with the date indicated in the contract itself. Therefore, if the insured risk takes place within the term when the insurance premium or its first instalment should be paid, the contract is valid irrespective of whether the insured risk takes place before or after the payment of the insurance premium.

The second sentence of this provision, however, refers to other paragraphs of this Article. Article $7.^{2}(2)$ and (3) ICA deals with the situation of the late payment of the insurance premium or its first instalment by allowing the insurer the choice to accept such late payment or not.

The last paragraph of the discussed Article clearly envisages the principle of the real contract by regulation of the situation if the insured risk takes place after the late payment of the insurance premium or its first instalment. The first sentence of that provision states:

> If the insurance premium or its first part is paid after the time period for payment determined in the insurance contract and if until the day of payment of the insurance premium or its first part an insured risk has occurred, it shall be considered that the insurance contract has not entered into effect and the insurer has a duty to notify the policyholder on invalidity of the contract and to reimburse the paid insurance premium or its first part.

As one may observe from this quoted regulation, it contains a mandatory legal norm precluding the choice for the insurer in the discussed situation.

119. The Insurance Contract Act does not envisage *any form requirements* for the conclusion of an insurance contract which, therefore, could be concluded in any form (with an exception of specific insurance contracts such as a motor insurance contract which is regulated by specific legal acts). Insurance contracts are usually concluded in written form in Latvian insurance practice as elsewhere; however, one may not exclude absence of written form.

Previously, before the amendments were introduced to the Insurance Contract Act in 2007, Article 7(1) ICA had provided for written form requirement for an insurance contract to enter into force. However, the written form requirement was abandoned in 2007 when the discussed amendments were introduced to that Act. The fact that Insurance Contract Act does not request written form for an insurance contract to enter into force anymore is also testified by a provision stating that an insurance contract is valid without signatures of the parties.[99] Another evidence relates to the situation allowed by the Insurance Contract Act when an insurance contract

99. Article 13(3) ICA.

is concluded by distance means. If an insurance policy is not issued upon conclusion of an insurance contract by distance means, the insurance policy may be issued to policyholder on its request later.[100] Such regulation approves the conclusion that the insurance contract may enter into force even if it is not expressed in written form.

120. As regards *writing requirements* of insurance contracts, neither general civil law regulation nor insurance contract regulation provides extensive writing requirements concerning an insurance contract text.

121. Latvian general civil law regulation does not envisage special requirements concerning a contract writing. Therefore, contract parties may exploit freedom of contracts for drafting contract text subject to civil law principles such as the good faith principle or mandatory legal norms. An exception is provided for in the case of contracts concluded by a seller or a provider of service with a consumer if a contract is based on standard terms, which is subject to writing requirements set out in Article 6 of the Consumer Protection Rights Act in conjuncture with the Unfair Terms Directive.

122. At the same time, writing of an insurance contract is subject to special requirements which are provided by insurance contract law in respect of state language requirements and inclusion of certain elements into an insurance contract.

123. In the beginning, it should be noted that as an exception from freedom of contracts, insurance contract may contain such provisions which are related to the insurance nature as such. As it was noted by the Latvian Supreme Court in this regard, the Insurance Contract Act:

> does not prevent the parties to freely agree on provisions of the insurance contract, but they may not come into conflict with provisions of the law which characterise the essence of the insurance contract, which generally envisage rights and obligations of the insured, the policyholder and the insurer both before the conclusion of the insurance contract and during its validity period as well as provide the consequences of their non-fulfilment and pre-conditions for non-fulfilment or invalidity of the contract.[101]

124. As regards writing requirements, Article 6(1) ICA provides that provisions of an insurance contract must be clear and comprehensible. However, the Insurance Contract does not provide any penalty for non-observance of such duty on the part of the insurer considering that insurance contracts usually are based on standard contract terms. It could be assumed that application of the good faith principle in this situation could lead to exploitation of the *contra proferentem* interpretation rule.

100. Article 7.[1](2) ICA.
101. Judgement of the Latvian Supreme Court dated 14 Feb. 2014 in Case No SKC-17/2014.

For comparison, Article 6(2) of the Consumer Rights Protection Act contains similar requirement for writing standard contract terms 'in plain and comprehensible language'. At the same time, Article 6(2.^{1}) of that Act provides a penalty for non-compliance with that requirement by pointing out to the *contra proferentem* interpretation rule. These rules would be applicable in the case of insurance contracts if either a policyholder or an insured person (i.e., a person who has a claim against the insurer for collection of insurance redress) is considered as a consumer. In one recent case, the Latvian Supreme Court interpreted the insurance contract which contained standard contract terms by using the *contra proferentem* interpretation rule in favour of a consumer in the dispute over collection of insurance redress.[102]

125. Likewise, violation of the requirement indicated in Article 6(1) ICA could also lead to application of regulation on unfair commercial practices, especially considering lack of professional diligence.

126. Another requirement relates to the *state language* requirement. The first sentence of Article 6.^{1} ICA provides that an insurance contract shall be prepared and entered into using the official language. As one may notice from the very wording of this provision, especially from the use of the words 'prepared and entered', the state language requirement covers not only writing of an insurance contract text but also its conclusion which includes communication between the policyholder and the insurer. At the same, the second sentence of Article 6.^{1} ICA allows conclusion of an insurance contract in a foreign language, but in this situation, expression of intent of the policyholder must be indicated unmistakably in the insurance contract.

127. Further requirement relates to elements that shall be included in an insurance contract text if it is concluded in written form, which list is included in Article 6(2) ICA as well as Article 55(1) ICA in relation to personal insurance contracts. Liability for non-inclusion of these elements into the insurance contract text is on the part of the insurer. Article 94(2) of the Insurance and Reinsurance Act provides that in case if the requirements of Articles 6(2) and 55 ICA are not fulfilled, the supervision authority (FKTK) is entitled to impose on the insurer or the reinsurer a penalty of up to EUR 142,000.

128. As it is specially provided by Article 6(3) ICA, insurance contract parties may include other provisions into an insurance contract which comply with this Act and general provisions on transactions subject to requirements discussed above.

102. Judgement of the Latvian Supreme Court dated 4 Jul. 2017 in Case No SKC-243/2017.

Chapter 4. Term of an Insurance Contract

129. General civil law regulation included in the CL does not envisage general regulation in respect of a term for which a contract may be entered into. Within this regulation, one may conclude that contract parties may freely agree concerning the term for which a contract is concluded within the freedom of contracts. However, regulation of an insurance contract included in the Insurance Contract Act contains special norms concerning term of an insurance contract.

Latvia adheres to few such European countries which regulate *maximum term* for which an insurance contract may be entered into. Article 25(1) ICA repeats a rule arising from the principle of freedom of contract that the term of validity of an insurance contract shall be determined by agreement of the parties. However, this provision simultaneously lays down another rule on a maximum insurance contract term by providing that an insurance contract term may not exceed five years.

There are *three exceptions* from this regulation on maximum insurance contract term within the five-year period. Article 25(1) ICA provides itself the first exception by stating that such a maximum insurance contract limitation 'shall not be applicable to the total term of successively concluded insurance contracts'. Another exception is provided by Article 25(2) ICA by envisaging that this limitation does not apply for life insurance and health insurance as the maximum term of validity of a life insurance or health insurance contract shall not be limited. Last exception relates to terms for motor insurance contracts which are subject to terms in respect of different types of a motor insurance contracts laid down in the Motor Insurance Act.[103]

Above-mentioned regulation of a maximum term for an insurance contract does not cause significant problems in Latvian insurance practice. An exception could be that certain insurance law areas such as product liability or insurance of a variable interest rate (such as *Euribor*) against its rising for the whole term of validity of a mortgage contract (which is usually concluded in Latvia for fifteen years and more).

Minimum term or fixed term for an insurance contract is not provided statutorily except for different types of a motor insurance contract.[104] Likewise, *renewal term* for an insurance contract is not regulated at all and purely depends on contractual parties.

103. For motor insurance contract terms, *see* Ch. 2, Part IV of this monograph below.
104. *Ibid.*

Chapter 5. Duties of a Policyholder (Insured)

130. The duties of a policyholder as another party to an insurance contract are generally provided by mandatory norms of the Insurance Contract Act and are further specified in a particular insurance contract. The general regulation of these duties is provided by Chapter V ICA. However, one should take into account that other duties are included in other norms of the Insurance Contract Act, for instance, concerning changes in initial information if they increase probability of the risks insured (Article 16 ICA discussed below in this chapter).

131. Duties of the policyholder may be considered as pre-contractual in reporting information on insurable object in relation to risks being insured (i.e., the so-called initial information); contractual as regarding payment of insurance premium, reporting about changes in the initial information if probability of the insured risk arose during the operational time of the contract; and duties in the case of occurrence of an insured risk that should be distinguished separately from other contractual duties.

132. The pre-contractual and contractual duties of a policyholder will be reviewed further separately. It should be taken into account that fulfilment of these duties refers not only to policyholder but also to the insured.

§1. Pre-contractual Duties

133. The basic obligation during the pre-contractual stage on the part of a policyholder refers to the reporting of all material facts which concern an object to be insured in relation to risks being insured. These facts are covered by the term 'initial information' employed by the Insurance Contract Act. The duty to report initial information and the consequences of non-fulfilment of that duty is subject to regulation provided by that Act.

134. Article 5(1) ICA lays down the characterisation of the duty for providing initial information. Its wording should be quoted here in full and is as follows:

> By entering into a contract, a policyholder or an insured person has a duty to provide all the information regarding the circumstances the insurer has requested which information is necessary for the insurer in order to assess the probability of the occurrence of insurance risk and is important for entering into an insurance contract.

135. As it can be observed from this quote, Latvia shares the approach of *reporting all material facts* and *does not accept the questionnaire approach* which refers to reporting such facts which are requested by the insurer in writing. It means that all material information concerning an insurable object in respect of risks to be insured shall be submitted by the policyholder based on the utmost good faith principle and shall be disclosed fully. This provision, therefore, allows (and it is usually used in Latvian insurance practice) the section in an insurance questionnaire which is titled 'Other Information'. This questionnaire section, if used, allows for insurers to shift the knowledge of material facts necessary for evaluation of the insurance of a particular insurance object in respect of risks to be insured completely to the policyholder.

136. Therefore, Article 5(1) ICA leaves significant burden on a policyholder to be capable of knowing himself or herself which facts are material and, therefore, shall be reported. Only one exception from this situation is provided by the Insurance Contract Act when a particular material fact shall be reported which refers to previously concluded insurance contracts. Article 5(4) ICA provides in this regard that a policyholder or the insured person has a duty to notify an insurer regarding other contracts in effect he or she is aware of, which pertain to the same insurance object.

137. Latvian courts have understood this duty under this provision broadly and were not, as far as the publicly available Latvian Supreme Court practice is concerned, inclined to shift this burden, at least partially, on the shoulders of the insurer.

138. The policyholder's duty to disclose initial information does not deprive insurers from their right to inspect an insurance object independently both before the conclusion of an insurance contract and during its operational time. This situation explicitly is regulated by Article 14(2) ICA which provides:

> Prior to entering into an insurance contract and during the operation thereof the insurer has the right in accordance with the procedures set out in the insurance contract to inspect the insurance object in order to ascertain that changes in the initial information have not occurred.

139. This insurer's right is widely and usually employed by Latvian insurers in the case of insurance of motor vehicles travelling on land in property insurance (the so-called Casco (casualty and collision) insurance or hull insurance).

140. Article 5(2) ICA explicitly admits that the duty for reporting initial information, i.e., 'the veracity of the information provided' should be fulfilled by both a policyholder and the insured.

141. If initial information which was requested in writing by an insurer was not reported and the insurer has entered into an insurance contract, the insurer, as explicitly admitted by Article 5(3) ICA, may not use the fact of non-provision of information as a reason for the termination of the contract or amending its provisions. There is an exception to this rule which is provided by that provision, namely, in the case if requested information was not submitted due to bad faith or gross negligence either by a policyholder or an insured.

§2. CONTRACTUAL DUTIES EXCEPT DUTIES IN THE CASE OF AN INSURED EVENT [PAYMENT OF PREMIUM]

142. There are *three main duties* of the policyholder and the insured to be discussed (the third is discussed in the next sub-chapter): (1) payment of insurance premium; (2) reporting about changes in the initial information in case if probability of the insured risk is increased during the operational time of the contract; and (3) obligations in the case of occurrence of an insured risk.

143. As regards the duty of payment of insurance premium, this duty is provided by Article 18(1) ICA which is worth to be quoted in full:

> A policyholder has a duty to pay insurance premium in the manner, time periods and amount specified in the contract.

144. As it could be observed from the wording of Article 18(1) ICA, the amount of the insurance premium and its payment term depend on the terms of a particular insurance contract. Neither the current nor previous wordings of the Insurance Contract Act have ever provided for any regulation of the amount of insurance premium or envisaged any regulation for its payment terms. Similarly, special legal norms in other legal acts concerning specific insurance contracts such as a motor insurance contract or a marine insurance contract do not also provide such regulation. An exception to this situation is the regulation which existed before Latvia acceded to the EU and abandoned before the accession which provided material control on both insurance contract terms and amounts of insurance premiums.[105]

145. Article 18(1) ICA clearly envisages that insurance premium can consist only of money and, therefore, cannot be expressed in any other manner. As an example, one may mention lease fee which pursuant to Article 2119 CL could be expressed either in money or other things, such as movables (for instance, in shoes, as admitted by the Latvian Supreme Court in one of its reviewed cases).

146. This provision, however, does allow to use different forms of payment of insurance premium. In practice, insurance premium can be expressed as a lump sum payment or in instalments (either in certain sums or a percentage from the total amount of the insurance premium) each payable in a certain time period (periods).

147. The consequences of non-payment of insurance premium in full may lead to two outcomes depending on the choice of the insurer: (1) termination of the insurance contract as provided by Article 18(2) ICA by initiative of the insurer or (2) its collection in court proceedings. The procedure for termination of the insurance in the former situation is set out separately in Article 19 ICA. Insurers in Latvia usually prefer to proceed with the first option. An exception to this choice exists in the

105. For a discussion of this issue, *see* Ch. 3, Part II above.

case of motor insurance contracts which are consensual contracts by entering into force irrespective of the payment of insurance premium.[106]

148. Though the Insurance Contract Act explicitly provides that duty of payment of insurance premium falls with a policyholder as it could be observed from Article 18(1) ICA quoted above, this duty could be simultaneously viewed as a duty of the insured as well who would otherwise lose the insurance cover.

149. Another contractual duty of a policyholder relates to *changes in the initial information* submitted earlier in the pre-contractual stage which took place after conclusion of the insurance contract. The Latvian Supreme Court has stated in one of its recent judgments that initial information shall be distinguished from changes in initial information as it involves two different standards of evaluation of duties of a policyholder.

150. Changes in initial information are treated in the Insurance Contract Act separately in Chapter III ICA (containing three articles, namely Articles 14–16 ICA) whose title is 'Increase and Decrease of Probability of Occurrence of Insurance Risk'.

151. The concept 'changes in initial information' is used just once in the text of the Insurance Contract Act, and it appears in the title of Article 14 ICA. The understanding of that term, however, is undoubtedly provided in Article 14(1) ICA which is quoted below:

> During the operation of an insurance contract, except the case of a person's life assurance and health insurance, in conformity with that laid down in Section 5 of this Law, the insured person or policyholder has a duty to notify in writing as soon as this is possible the insurer of all circumstances he or she is aware of which may considerably increase the probability of the occurrence of insurance risk or amount of potential losses.

152. As it could be noticed from the quote above, the changes in initial information concept refer to 'all circumstances he or she is aware of which may considerably increase the probability of the occurrence of insurance risk or amount of potential losses'. These 'all circumstances' refer to material facts concerning the insured risk (risks) in relation to the insured object by covering two situations: either (1) 'increase the probability of the occurrence of insurance risk' or (2) 'amount of potential losses'. Similarly, as in the case of initial information, the duty to report of such material facts relates to both a policyholder and an insured, including the burden of knowledge of facts which are material in a particular situation.

106. For discussion of Latvian motor insurance law, *see* Part IV below.

153. Two exceptions from that duty are provided by the discussed provision, namely such a duty does not exist in case if a life insurance or health insurance contract is concluded. Another exception regarding accident insurance may be deduced from the whole structure of the Insurance Contract Act and the very term of initial information. Similarly, personal insurance in general should be outside of regulation of changes in initial information.

154. The Insurance Contract Act distinguishes two kinds of changes of the initial information in relation to duties of a policyholder, and both of them relate to the probability of occurrence of the insured risk, i.e., increase and decrease of probability of occurrence of the insured risk. Both these situations are regulated under the Latvian Insurance Contract Act in a separate manner and, therefore, they will be discussed separately.

155. The duties of a policyholder and rights of an insurer in the case of increase of probability of occurrence of the insured risk are regulated by Article 16 ICA. Article 16 ICA distinguishes two different situations: the first situation covers compliance of the policyholder with that duty, and the second covers non-compliance with that duty.

156. In the case of the former situation, when the policyholder has reported to the insurer changes in initial information, the insurer is entitled to either (1) insist of introducing amendments into the insurance contract terms (Article 16(1) ICA); (2) termination of the insurance contract depending on the fact whether the insurer would or would not conclude that contract with knowledge of changes in initial information (Article 16(2)–(3) ICA); or to avoid any of the two above activities by agreeing with the changes in initial information (Article 16(4) ICA). If the insured risk takes place before any of the first two activities are undertaken, but the duty of reporting the changes in initial information was observed, this fact cannot lead to refusal of insurance redress (Article 16(5) ICA).

157. In the latter situation, when the policyholder has failed to report to the insurer changes in initial information, it involves consequences of that failure (Article 16 (6)–(8) ICA).

§3. Duties in the Case of Insured Event

158. Contractual duties in the case of insured event will be discussed separately within this sub-chapter. These duties are governed by Article 21 ICA, and they are regulated by referring only to the insured person. An obvious deficiency is the case of life insurance where such duty should refer to beneficiary but not to heirs of the insured.

The first and the most important duty of the insured person after he or she found out about materialisation of the insured risk may be found in Article 21(1) ICA, which provides for a duty 'to notify the insurer about the fact of the occurrence of the insured risk'. This duty shall be fulfilled, as it is provided by this provision, 'without delay, at the earliest opportunity'. Another related duty concerns precautionary measures which are also provided by the discussed provision by stating to 'take all appropriate measures in order to reduce the losses'.

Concerning materialisation of the insured risk, Article 21(2) ICA envisages that the insured person is under the duty to submit the insurer necessary documents and information in order to allow the insurer to carry out assessment of the insured risk, including determination and quantification of the amount of damages. The last sentence of Article 21(2) ICA also makes it clear that there could be other duties to be fulfilled depending on the insurance contract in question. In this regard, this provision states that the insured person is obliged to 'perform other duties provided for in the insurance contract'.

At the same time, Article 21(3) ICA clarifies that the notification of information (and obviously also documents) concerning the insured event may not be considered as a violation by the insured person or the insured.

Chapter 6. Duties of the Insurer

159. In contrast to duties of a policyholder (which could be simultaneously attributed also to the insured as mentioned above), duties of an insurer are envisaged in both insurance contract regulation included in the Insurance Contract Act and supervision regulation provided by the Insurance and Reinsurance Act. Duties of the insurer are regulated by Latvian insurance contract law poorly except life insurance and only because of the impact of EU law.

160. The duties of the insurer may be classified depending on the classification of insurance into life and non-life insurance: these duties are either as general duties applying both to non-life insurance and life insurance or as special duties depending on the type of insurance, i.e., non-life or life insurance. Similarly, as in the case of the policyholder, Latvian insurance contract law divides duties of the insurer into pre-contractual and contractual duties by providing regulation concerning both types of duties. However, regulation of pre-contractual duties is formalistic as it is further revealed.

161. As regards pre-contractual duties of the insurer in non-life insurance, these duties are regulated by both the Insurance Contract Act and the Insurance and Reinsurance Act.

162. The Insurance Contract Act provides for the duty of an insurer to inform a policyholder about certain insurance contract elements such as dispute resolution or applicable law. In this regard, Article 3(3) ICA provides that prior to entering into an insurance contract an insurer has an obligation to inform a policyholder of such procedures as the examination in an extrajudicial way of complaints and disputes which might arise from the insurance contract. This duty, as it is provided by that provision itself, refers only in relation to such a policyholder who is a natural person. Furthermore, Article 2(7) ICA envisages that prior to entering into an insurance contract an insurer has a duty to inform a policyholder (irrespective of whether he or she is a natural person, legal person or a partnership) about the applicable law in respect of an insurance contract in question.

163. In addition, Chapter XXII of the Insurance and Reinsurance Act contains rules concerning information that shall be notified before the conclusion of an insurance contract and provides that the insurer must inform the policyholder about certain issues which are dealt separately in non-life insurance and life insurance.

164. One of the pre-contractual duties of the insurer with respect to non-life insurance relates to notifying certain information such as the home country of the insurer, its legal address, contact information and the natural person who acts on behalf of the insurer. The first two elements shall be stated in every document submitted to the policyholder (Article 179(1)–(2) of the Insurance and Reinsurance

Act). These pre-contractual duties solely apply in the case of mass risks considering that none of them apply in respect of large risk insurance. [107]

165. Furthermore, the insurer has the duty to find out demands and needs of the client, i.e., the policyholder.[108] At the same time, the insurer is under the duty to explain the essence of deductibles and overinsurance or underinsurance to the policyholder if it may affect the needs of the policyholder.[109] However, significance of this duty is seriously undermined by the fact that the signature of the policyholder is sufficient for establishing the fulfilment of that duty.[110] Based on this regulation, Latvian insurers usually avoid explaining the essence of overinsurance and underinsurance in Latvian insurance practice by relying on the signature of the policyholder on the insurance contract which contains a provision that the insurer has explained the essence of deductibles and overinsurance or underinsurance to the policyholder.

166. Duties of the insurer in life insurance are dealt separately by the Insurance and Reinsurance Act in its Article 180. This Article envisages information that should be included in a life insurance contract and amendments to this information that should be notified to the policyholder. Similarly, as in the case of non-life insurance, the signature of the policyholder is sufficient evidence that such information was notified as also stated by Article 181 of the above Act.

167. Pre-contractual duties also cover writing requirements of insurance contracts which are envisaged in the case of the insurer. Article 6(1) ICA lays down general rule for writing insurance contracts as '[p]rovisions of an insurance contract must be clear and comprehensible'. It is the insurer's duty to include at least those details into insurance policies which are provided by Article 6(2) ICA in respect of all insurance contracts, but Article 55(1) ICA provides special rules for personal insurance contracts. Liability for non-compliance with that duty is provided by the insurance supervision regulation. Indeed, Article 94(2) of the Insurance and Reinsurance Act provides that FKTK may impose on the insurer a fine of up to EUR 14,200 if provisions under Articles 6(2), 24.[1] (duties of the insurer provided by this Article is discussed below) and 55 of the Insurance Contract Act are not fulfilled. At the same time, Article 6(3) does not prohibit insurance contract parties to introduce other contractual provisions if they do not contradict mandatory statutory provisions.

168. A special regulation is provided in Article 6.[1] ICA concerning the language of an insurance contract. This Article provides that an insurance contract shall be drafted and entered into using the official language, i.e., Latvian. Though this Article does not provide which person has the duty to observe that rule, however, from

107. None of these duties apply in respect of large risk insurance (Article 179(3) Insurance and Reinsurance Act) as defined by Art. 194 Insurance and Reinsurance Act.
108. Article 179(4) Insurance and Reinsurance Act.
109. Article 179(5) Insurance and Reinsurance Act.
110. Article 181 Insurance and Reinsurance Act.

insurance contract regulation in general, it may be assumed that this duty falls upon the insurer and should not be attributed to the policyholder. At the same time, the Insurance Contract Act allows to conclude the insurance contract in foreign language. However, this option is possible only if a policyholder wishes to do so and such expression of intent of the policyholder should be unmistakably indicated in the insurance contract.

169. After conclusion of the insurance contract, the insurer shall inform the policyholder as well as the insured about the changes in information concerning the insurer, which is necessary for the fulfilment of contractual obligations by the policyholder (insured person) such as legal form, name, contact telephones, contact addresses and contact persons and similar.

170. Contractual duties of the insurer mainly refer to occurrence of the insured risk regulated under Articles 24 and 24.[1] ICA, discussed further in this sub-chapter. At the same time, other contractual duties on the part of the insurer, such as the duty to inform about taxation regime in personal insurance contracts (Article 55(2) ICA), may be established, discussed further in this sub-chapter.

171. Duties in relation to the occurrence of the insured risk may be divided into two groups depending on the character of these duties.

172. The *first* group covers duties of examining the *circumstances of the occurrence of the insured risk.* Article 24(1) ICA envisages the general duty of the insurer to provide insurance redress in the case of the occurrence of the insurable event. Therefore, it is for the insurer to prove any circumstances which may release the insurer from the obligation to pay insurance redress (Article 24(6) ICA).

173. At the same time, Article 24(2) ICA provides for the following duties concerning occurrence of the insured risk which would be purposeful to quote in full:

1) reject or approve a claim issued on the basis of the insurance contract without verifying the occurrence of insurance risk;
2) refuse to pay insurance redress without verifying all the available information;
3) refuse to pay insurance compensation [insurance redress – author's remark] within the time period determined in the insurance contract if evidence with regard to the occurrence of insurable event is received;
4) pay insurance compensation [insurance redress – author's remark] if the occurrence of insurance risk has been caused by the bad faith of a policyholder, insured person, beneficiary or a third party. In such cases, the insurer shall not reimburse the paid up insurance premiums.

174. As one may observe from the very wording of this provision, these duties are to be considered as imperative and apply to every insurer irrespective of insurance contract terms.

175. A special regulation is provided if *the insurer refuses payment of insurance redress*. In this situation, as Article 24(7) ICA provides, the insurer shall send a motivated written notification to the policyholder and the insured person within ten days after making the decision.

176. As regards the insurer's decision to provide insurance redress, a special provision is provided if the policyholder is a natural person.

177. In this situation, Article 24(8) ICA states that the insurer shall pay insurance redress in a particular time period, i.e., within fifteen days from the date when the decision to pay the insurance compensation was made. Two exceptions from payment of insurance redress within that period are provided in this situation: the first exception refers to the situation when payment of the insurance redress should be provided either in the form of periodical payments or provision of secured services; the second exception applies when the insurer and the insured (victim, beneficiary) have agreed to other terms.

178. The *second* group of duties refer to *adoption of a decision* for payment or non-payment of insurance redress. The time period for adoption of such a decision is provided in the case of natural persons in Article 24.[1] ICA. According to this Article, an insurer shall within one month from the date of receipt of all the documents determined in an insurance contract make a decision on the payment of insurance compensation. As it could be observed from this regulation, regulation of such term is ambiguous as insurers may request again and again certain documents and continue assessment of the insured risk for an uncertain period of time. Such situation may be the reason why insured persons chose to submit claims for collection of insurance redress in the court considering the fact that a considerable time period has passed since submitting a claim to the insurer and no decision of the insurer is adopted.

179. In addition, the insurance supervision regulation provides that the insurer shall issue documents which substantiate the decision of the insurer on providing or refusal to provide insurance redress to a person who may claim insurance redress.[111] Likewise, the insurer is under the duty to issue a motivated reply within one month to the request of the policyholder, the insured or the person who may claim insurance redress concerning a service incompatible with insurance contract provisions.[112]

180. Special contractual duties are provided for with respect to personal insurance contracts irrespective of their type, i.e., in respect of all life, health and accident insurance contracts. Article 55(2) ICA provides that if the term of personal insurance contract exceeds one year, the insurer shall inform the policyholder and insured person in writing regarding taxation regime and its amendments in relation to insurance premiums and insurance redress and gratuities (bonuses) granted at

111. Article 182(1)–(3) Insurance and Reinsurance Act.
112. Article 182(4) Insurance and Reinsurance Act.

least once every twelve months. As one may observe from this provision, this duty on the part of the insurer applies only in case if the term of a personal insurance contract exceeds one year, but not to such a personal insurance contract concluded for one year or less.

Chapter 7. Insurance and Third Parties (Third-Party Beneficiary Clauses, Direct Action, etc.)

181. The legal institute of third parties' claims and its regulation plays a considerable role in the regulation of whole insurance law area. Latvian insurance contract law addresses third parties' claims, yet this regulation is insufficient and fragmentary.

182. The Insurance Contract Act admits third-party insurance, i.e., insurance in favour of third parties. Indeed, the legal definition of a policyholder provides that a person concludes an insurance contract 'for the benefit of himself or herself or of another person' (Article 1(6) ICA). This reflects one of the classifications of insurance law based on insurable interest, i.e., either first-party or third-party insurance, which is familiar to Latvian insurance contract law. Third-party insurance is further regulated in the legal definition of the term 'insured'. The term 'insured' is defined as a person 'who has the insurable interest and for the benefit of whom the insurance contract has been entered into' (Article 1(12) ICA). As one may observe from the legal definition of the term 'insured', it contains a reference to a person who must demonstrate insurable interest, i.e., the insured.

183. At the same time, the Insurance Contract Act does not provide any further regulation of third parties' claims, except direct action against the insurer which is discussed further separately. Such a lack of regulation has caused disputes which were solved by Latvian courts in rather specific manner.

184. One such dispute referred to a hull insurance contract in respect of the ship *Sventa* and concerned the situation whether insurance contract parties could amend the person of the insured after conclusion of the insurance contract if this contract was concluded in favour of a third party (i.e., third-party insurance). In effect, such activities change the third-party insurance contract concluded initially to the first-party insurance contract. In the *Sventa* case, Latvian courts took into account insufficient regulation of third parties' insurance in the Insurance Contract Act and applied general regulation of contracts within the law of obligations. This regulation, however, is still based on the Roman private law conception 'alteri stipulari nemo potest' which rejects possibility for a contract to be binding to a third person. Therefore, Latvian courts in the *Sventa* case established that if an insurance contract was concluded in favour of a third party, this contract becomes binding upon the third party, when he or she accedes this contract.

185. Similarly, Latvian courts admitted the free choice of insurance contract parties to change the person of the insured even in the case of third-party insurance, in other words – to change freely a third-party insurance contract to a first-party insurance contract without the consent of the third party in question in whose favour the insurance contract was concluded.[113]

113. Judgment of the Latvian Supreme Court of the Republic of Latvia dated 9 Jan. 2008. in Case No

186. It should be mentioned that the application of the good faith principle anchored in the very Article 1 CL could produce a different result in this case precluding the interests of the third party. However, Latvian courts did not consider the case from the perspective of the good faith principle.

187. In comparison, change of a beneficiary in personal insurance contracts is explicitly regulated under the Latvian Insurance Contract Act. Article 53 (1) ICA grants the rights to the policyholder[114] to indicate any person or persons to be beneficiary or to substitute these persons with other persons just by an application to the insurer who cannot even object to such changes.

188. Direct action is regulated solely on the basis of Article 50 ICA which refers to 'Right of the Third Party to Bring Action in Court':

> A third party has the right to bring an action to the court directly against an insurer in the cases laid down by laws and regulations, and the insurer has the right to contest justification of the brought action.

189. As one may observe from the wording of this provision, it applies only to civil liability as the term 'third party' is understood as 'a person in the civil liability insurance for whom the payment of the insurance compensation is provided' (Article 1 (21) ICA). If a civil liability contract is concluded, a third party may claim insurance redress only if a special legal act provides for such direct action as it is explicitly referred to in Article 50 ICA quoted above.

190. As far as the anonymised database of court practice of Latvian courts is concerned, two cases could be identified which led to the application of Article 50 ICA. One case refers to compulsory professional civil liability insurance of security firms in which Latvian courts established that there exists direct action against the insurer on the basis of the Security Activity Act.[115] Another case refers to compulsory professional civil liability insurance of court bailiffs where the first instance court (the case was heard only at the first instance) reviewed the claim against an insurer who insured civil liability of a court bailiff and allowed a direct action in the situation when the Court Bailiffs Act does not even provide for such direct action.[116] Interestingly, none of these proceedings resulted in a decision in favour of the victim since civil liability of the insured was not established which precluded fulfilment of the insurance contract.

SKC-4/2008, in: Latvijas Republikas Augstākās tiesas Senāta Civillietu departamenta spriedumi un lēmumi 2008. R.: Tiesu namu aentūra, 2009, 185–195. lpp.

114. Please note that the official translation of the Act erroneously uses the term 'insured' instead of the 'policyholder'.

115. Judgment of Riga Regional Court dated 4 Dec. 2013 in civil Case No C30524012 (appealed, cassation proceedings were refused).

116. Judgment of Riga city Vidzeme district court of 24 Mar. 2015 in civil Case No C30809912 (not appealed).

Chapter 8. Duty to Pay Interest

191. Failure of fulfilment of obligations is subject to different legal consequences expressed in remedies available for the creditor against the debtor who failed to perform his or her obligation. One such consequence relates to the duty to pay statutory interest which arises on the basis of law (with an exception that if an insurance contract provides for a contractual interest. As this is usually not provided by insurance contracts in Latvian insurance practice, such a possibility will not be discussed separately). This duty is considered in Latvian civil law as one of the so-called quasi-contracts which arise 'pursuant to law' (Article 1402 CL). The duty to pay statutory interest applies also in the case of failure to fulfil obligations within an insurance contract; however, it is subject to peculiar approaches developed by Latvian courts.

192. Duty to cover statutory interest may arise in insurance contract relationships in relation to different claims to be brought either by insurance contract parties against each other or by insured persons against the insurer. The Insurance Contract Act does not provide any regulation on duty to cover statutory interest. Therefore, general regulation for interest included in the CL shall be applicable. However, lack of such special legal norms on statutory interest in insurance contract relationships has caused problems for application of statutory interest in certain occasions – specifically, concerning failure to provide insurance redress.

193. General regulation of statutory interest contains, inter alia, a list of grounds for claiming statutory interest from a debtor. This list consisting of five grounds is included in Article 1759 CL. Specifically, Article 1759(1) CL provides late-payment interest as one such ground which shall be paid even if not specifically agreed to, on the basis of law, regarding delayed payment of a debt, even though the debt itself may be interest free. As one may notice from the very wording of Article 1759(1) CL, it envisages duty to pay late-payment interest (being one of the grounds of claiming statutory interest) in the case of any late payment of debt. Similarly, late-payment interest applies also to late payments within an insurance contract.

194. As regards a policyholder's duty to pay insurance premium, duty to pay statutory interest may arise in the case of late or non-payment of insurance premium. At the same time, in the case of insured persons, duty to pay statutory interest may arise either for insurance redress which was not paid in due time, or in the case of refusal of payment of insurance redress if the court later satisfies the claim for payment of insurance redress.

195. However, Latvian court practice has taken the peculiar standpoint in the case of duty to pay statutory interest if a court establishes that refusal to provide insurance redress was ungrounded. This situation concerns interpretation of Article 1759(1) CL. According to well-settled court practice of Latvian courts, duty to pay statutory interest in this situation does not exist. As it is established by the Latvian

Supreme Court, which forms well-settled court practice (judicature), interest is payable for each delay of payment of the debt, but:

> such delay does not take place because no decision has been taken on the payment of the insurance redress, but the refusal to pay the redress may not be classified as a debt, although the court has later recognized that the insured event has taken place.[117]

196. This Latvian courts' approach, which was criticised in Latvian legal literature,[118] may be explained by the fact that Latvian insurance law neither provides a special norm for duty to pay statutory interest for late payment of insurance redress nor a precise term for payment of insurance redress. Specifically, such a term is not established also by Article 24.[1] ICA in relation to natural persons as it allows to request additional documents for an indefinite period of time. In the situation concerning term, good faith principle may be applicable; however, Latvian courts, at least if publicly available court practice of the Latvian Supreme Court is concerned, has not proceed this way.

197. The discussed Latvian courts' approach extends to motor insurance except when an insurer or the Latvian Motor Insurers' Bureau has not provided insurance redress after the term prescribed by the Motor Insurance Act (set out by Article 39(3) and (4) Motor Insurance Act).

---

117. Judgment of the Latvian Supreme Court of the Republic of Latvia dated 17 Dec. 2003 in Case No SKC-610.

118. Rone D. Likumisko procentu piedziņa apdrošināšanas atlīdzības izmaksas lietās. Grām.: Juridiskās zinātnes aktuālās problēmas. Rakstu krājums. R.: Zvaigzne ABC, 2012, 7–20. lpp.

Chapter 9. Termination of the Insurance Contract (End of Term, Disappearance of the Risk, Cancelling of the Contract, Statute of Limitations, etc.)

198. Termination of the insurance contract may take place in several situations provided either by the general law of obligations or by Latvian insurance contract law.

199. The first and the most common situation refers to the expiry of the term of the insurance contract. The Insurance Contract Act does not explicitly provide for such obvious possibility for termination of the insurance contract, yet it may be deduced from provisions included in Articles 25–26 ICA.

200. Likewise, the Insurance Contract Act distinguishes several situations when a concluded insurance contract may be invalid or terminated before expiry of its term.

201. The first situation refers to the so-called absolute grounds of non-validity of an insurance contract. These grounds cover the situation in which an insurance contract has been entered into force. For instance, at least one of the essential elements of an insurance contract on the basis of the legal definition of an insurance contract is missing (Article 1 (5) ICA). Similarly, the Insurance Contract Act specifically provides that the insurance contract is not valid if either insurable risk or insurable interest does not exist at any time during the validity term of the insurance contract.[119]

202. Another situation refers to cases when an insurance contract may be terminated upon the initiative of one of the insurance contract parties.

203. As regards a policyholder, the Insurance Contract Act does not allow for the policyholder to unilaterally withdraw from the validly concluded insurance contract. An exception is provided in the case of life insurance. If a life insurance contract is concluded, a policyholder may unilaterally withdraw from such a contract, and he or she is entitled to a special kind of payment called a surrender value as defined by Article 1(22) ICA.

204. A different situation takes place in the case of an insurer who has much broader possibilities for termination of the insurance contract on its own initiative. Two situations should be distinguished depending on the fact whether this initiative is based on illegal activity of a policyholder or insured persons.

205. One the one hand, the insurer may exploit a right of unilateral withdrawal from the insurance contract on the basis of an illegal activity of the policyholder or insured persons.

119. Articles 10 (1) and 11 (1) ICA.

206. The first straightforward situation refers to non-payment of insurance premium if it shall be paid in instalments (on a condition that the first instalment of the insurance premium was duly paid). This situation involves failure of fulfilment of one of the duties on the part of a policyholder. In this situation, as it was discussed previously, the insurer may unilaterally withdraw from the insurance contract as per the procedure provided by Article 19 ICA. This situation shall be differentiated from the situation of late non-payment of the insurance premium if it should be paid in the full amount or late non-payment of the first instalment of the insurance premium. In the latter situation, the insurer may refuse to accept such a late payment by reporting it to the policyholder within fifteen days from the moment of receiving such a payment (Article 7.2 ICA). The consequences of such a refusal lead to invalidity of an insurance contract.

207. Another situation refers to deception of an insurer by reporting initial information that is governed by Article 8 ICA. This Article provides that:

> If bad faith (Section 1641 of the Civil Law) or gross negligence (Section 1645 of the Civil Law) of a policyholder or the insured person has been the cause for deception of the insurer regarding the circumstances which it must know in order to assess the probability of occurrence of insurance risk, the insurance contract shall be declared null and void from the moment it has been entered into. The insurer shall not reimburse insurance premium paid.

208. As one may observe from this regulation, a set of conditions must be fulfilled for the insurer to employ the right to unilaterally withdraw from the insurance contract on the basis of this Article, namely bad faith or gross negligence; either by a policyholder or the insured; deception which shall take place in relation to 'the circumstances which it must know in order to assess the probability of occurrence of insurance risk'.

209. On the other hand, the insurer may have the right to unilaterally withdraw from the insurance contract on the basis of occurrence of certain events (legally significant facts) which are not related to illegal activity of the policyholder or insured persons. Regulation of such rights in the Insurance Contract Act is included in Articles 27–31 ICA; however, some of them are superfluous by overlapping with general regulation of termination of obligations as provided by the Latvian Civil Act. The following situations are covered by Articles 27–31 ICA:

- termination of an insurance contract between the date of entering into an insurance contract and the date of the coming into effect thereof (Article 27(1) ICA);
- termination of a life assurance or health insurance contract every year (Article 27(2) ICA);
- termination of an individual life assurance contract concluded for at least six-month term within fifteen days from the day of entering into such contract by a natural person (Article 27(3)–(4) ICA);

- termination of an insurance contract after occurrence of insurable event (Article 29 ICA);
- termination of an insurance contract in case of liquidation or insolvency of a policyholder (Article 30 ICA);
- termination of an insurance contract in the case of death of a policyholder (with an exception in the case of personal insurance) (Article 31 ICA).

210. The insurance contract loses its force by expiry of its term. The Insurance Contract Act does not provide that payment of insurance redress automatically terminates the insurance contract. Rather, as discussed above, payment of insurance redress could be considered as one of events which gives rise to the right of an insurer to unilaterally withdraw from the insurance contract. However, regulation of such rights in this Act is unnecessary due to the fact that the fulfilment of the contract already took place and, therefore, the contract is terminated on the basis of fulfilment of the obligations as provided by general regulation for termination of obligations envisaged by the Latvian Civil Act.

Chapter 10. Limitation Period (Prescription Period)

211. Regulation of the limitation period (prescription period) is provided for in Latvian civil law by the Law of Obligations Part of the Latvian Civil Act as one of the cases for termination of obligations rights. Regulation of limitation period envisages the general term of limitation period in Article 1895 CL. Article 1895 of the Latvian Civil Act states that:

> All obligation rights which have not been expressly exempted from the impact of [limitation] and the use of which is not by law subject to shorter terms, shall terminate if the party entitled to them does not use them within a ten-year time period.

As one may observe from this provision, the general term of limitation period is envisaged as ten years unless a shorter, i.e., special, term of limitation period is provided or obligations rights exist which are not subject to any limitation period. Likewise, the general limitation period is not applicable by operation of civil law principles, such as the good faith principle, in specific circumstances.

212. The Latvian Civil Act provides two examples for claims which are not subject to any limitation period, i.e., obligations rights registered in the Land Register, except ancillary rights arising from such rights for which the term has elapsed, and claims regarding verification of boundaries (Articles 1907 and 1908 CL). However, neither general regulation of limitation period nor Latvian insurance contract law provides for any claim concerning an insurance contract which is not subject to a limitation period.

213. Latvian insurance contract law envisages regulation for special terms of limitation period in respect of claims arising from an insurance contract. This regulation due to its incomplete character has led to a sparkling debate in Latvian insurance legal literature and response from Latvian courts. As regards regulation of limitation period in Latvian civil law, it should be distinguished between the general limitation period and special limitation periods in the case of certain claims or specific insurance contracts. Regulation of special terms of limitation period is included in Article 32 ICA and is based on the so-called two-phase system.

214. The first phase covers submitting a claim arising from an insurance contract to the insurer. This phase is explicitly regulated by Article 32 (1) and (2) ICA which provides special terms of limitation periods for that phase depending on a particular claim. For payment of insurance redress claims, a term of limitation period is provided, amounting to ten years for claims arising from life and liability insurance, but three years for other insurance types, i.e., property insurance and personal insurance except life insurance which is subject to the 10 years term of limitation period as indicated above. But the term of limitation period for other claims (such as repayment of insurance premium if any) is subject to the limitation period of two years.

215. The second phase, which occurs when unfavourable decision of the insurer could be disputed within the court, is not regulated by Article 32 ICA. This incomplete regulation led to a dispute as to which term of limitation period should be exploited. The Latvian Supreme Court decided to interpret Article 32 ICA in such a way that the general term of limitation period envisaged by the Latvian Civil Act should be applied, and it is ten years (Article 1895 CL).[120]

216. The interpretation provided by the Latvian Supreme Court in favour of the general term of limitation period was subject to different opinions in Latvian legal literature. There were insurance law commentators who disagreed with applying the general term of limitation period by arguing that the insurer's refusal to provide insurance redress should be subject to the same special term of limitation period as provided for submitting the claim to the insurer, i.e. it shall correspond to the special term exploited in the first phase.[121] Other legal commentators supported the opinion of the Latvian Supreme Court[122] which, as it was demonstrated before, is based on strict compliance with the regulation included in Article 32 ICA.

Special terms of limitation period are provided in other norms. There is the special term of limitation period for a recourse claim against the insured which is three years (Article 40 (8) ICA). The special term of limitation period for recourse claims against other persons is subject to the general term of limitation period envisaged by the Latvian Civil Act which is ten years as indicated above on the basis of the previously discussed approach of the Latvian Supreme Court concerning interpretation of Article 32 ICA.

217. Likewise, a special term of limitation period is provided for claims of victims arising from a motor insurance contract. Article 38(3) and (4) MIA contains regulation for specific terms of limitation period separately for damage to property and damage to person.

Article 38(3) MIA provides that:

> the right of a person who claims to receive insurance indemnity for the loss caused to the property of such person to raise a claim against the insurer or the Motor Insurers' Bureau shall cease if such right has not been claimed within a period of one year from the setting in of an insurable event.

However, Article 38(3) MIA states that:

> the right of a person who claims to receive insurance indemnity for bodily injuries to raise a claim against the insurer or Motor Insurers' Bureau shall cease if such right has not been claimed within three years from the setting in of an insurable event.

---

120. Judgment of the Latvian Supreme Court of the Republic of Latvia dated 12 Mar. 2014 in Case No SKC-184/2014.
121. Alfejeva J. Apdrošināšanas tiesības. R.: Turība, 2017, 78–80., 83.lpp.
122. Mantrovs V. Noilguma regulējums apdrošināšanas līgumā / Limitation period regulation in insurance contract, grām.: Tiesību efektivitāte postmodernā sabiedrībā: Latvijas Universitātes 73. zinātniskās konferences rakstu krājums. Rīga: Akadēmiskais apgāds, 2015, 75–80.lpp.

As one may observe from both these provisions, the special term of limitation period for pecuniary (material) claims is envisaged as one year but for 'damage caused to health', it is three years. It should be taken into account that the wording of the latter provision is ambiguous as it is not clear whether this special term of limitation period covers all non-pecuniary (non-material) damage caused as a result of a road traffic accident or just bodily injuries, i.e., 'damage caused to health' as it is explicitly envisaged by Article 38(3) MIA. It might be assumed that the second option should be preferred for the sake of clarity for victims as in this situation the general term of limitation period envisaged by the Latvian Civil Act (as discussed above) would apply for non-pecuniary damage other than 'damage caused to health'.

Part III. Property and Civil Liability Insurance

218. In this part, an overview is provided of special rules – whatever their nature: legal, customary, contractual, model forms, court practice, etc. – which govern property insurance (insurance against losses and damages in the terminology of the Insurance Contract Act) and civil liability insurance (liability insurance).

219. The specifics of Latvian insurance contract law relate to the fact that Latvian insurance contract law does not provide detailed regulation for different types of property and liability insurance. Rather, Latvian insurance contract law provides regulation of property and liability insurance in general allowing insurance contract parties to introduce specific contract terms in an insurance contract for specific property or liability insurance types (such as fire insurance, motor vehicle (*Casco* or hull) insurance, loss of benefits insurance, credit risk insurance and others). Likewise, regulation of property insurance and liability insurance is provided jointly in a separate chapter of the Insurance Contract Act, yet one may distinguish special rules in that regulation which are specifically applied in relation to either property insurance or liability insurance.

220. Considering this specific approach of Latvian insurance contract law, at the beginning general regulation common to both property and liability insurance is discussed, but afterwards specific rules concerning each of these insurance types are analysed.

Chapter 1. Property and Liability Insurance in General

221. Regulation of property insurance and liability insurance is provided in Chapter VII of the Insurance Contract Act. Common rules on both types of insurance are provided: they concern the compensation principle (indemnity principle in the terminology of the Latvian insurance contract law), multiple insurance which is closely related to the compensation principle and subrogation.

§1. Compensation Principle (Indemnity Principle)

222. One of the issues common for both property insurance and liability insurance relates to the indemnity principle, which is known in Latvian insurance law as the compensation principle. The compensation principle is one of the main insurance law principles in addition to such principles recognised also by Latvian insurance law as the insurable risk principle (i.e., no insurance without insurable risk), the insurable interest principle (i.e., no insurance without insurable interest) and the utmost good faith principle.[123]

223. The compensation principle is clarified at the legislative level in Latvian insurance contract law. Article 35 ICA (with the title 'Compensation Principle') is a leading Article for this issue:

> [I]n insurance against loss and damage and civil liability insurance, losses shall be compensated on the basis of the compensation principle. Insurance compensation paid may not exceed the loss caused to an insured person in an insurable event.

224. As one may observe from the structure and wording of Article 35 ICA, the nature of the compensation principle is reflected in the second sentence of that Article, while its first sentence provides the scope of application of this principle

The compensation principle envisages that insurance redress may not exceed the amount of damages caused to the insured person, i.e., a person who may claim provision of insurance redress from the insurer – an insured in property insurance, a victim in liability insurance and a beneficiary in personal insurance. In property insurance, it is expressed through the term 'value of the insured object', but in liability insurance it is through liability of the insured. As it arises from the first sentence of the commented Article, the compensation principle is applied in two insurance types, i.e., property insurance and liability insurance, excluding personal insurance. However, the Insurance Contract Act provides that the compensation principle may

123. For a review of principles of Latvian insurance contract law, *see* Ch. 1, Part II above.

be also applicable in personal insurance (life insurance, health insurance and accident insurance) if parties to a personal insurance contract so agrees.[124] Another provision, however, provides that life insurance is clearly outside of such choice.[125] In any case, application of the compensation principle in relation to personal insurance seems problematic because life insurance and accident insurance relate to non-material objects which cannot be valued in money, but health insurance covers different kinds of expenses without any relation to illegal activity of any person, especially in the case of medicinal exercises or massage services (to be covered depending on the terms of a health insurance contract).

§2. Multiple Insurance

225. Multiple insurance is not a rare situation in Latvian insurance practice. Multiple insurance characterises the situation when one and the same insurance object is insured against one and the same insured risk or risks. Usually this situation takes place when different insurers have concluded insurance contracts. Latvian insurance law provides regulation for multiple insurance for all insurance types.

226. Latvian insurance contract law does not allow an insurer involved in multiple insurance to reject insurance redress claim either fully or partially just based on the multiple insurance situation.[126] Rather, it provides for the possibility of establishing the amount of insurance redress within each insurance contract discussed in the next paragraph.

227. As regards property insurance, Article 37(1) ICA provides that if multiple insurance occurs in property insurance, 'each insurer shall pay insurance compensation in proportion to the amount determined by each insurance contract'. This provision, therefore, provides the proportionality principle based on the insured sums for establishing the amount of insurance redress. Though this provision refers to the situation when several insurers have concluded insurance contracts constituting multiple insurance, this regulation applies also to multiple insurance if it arises from two or more insurance contracts concluded by the single insurer.

228. A similar rule is provided in relation to liability insurance which is inserted in Article 37(2) ICA) by envisaging that the term 'liability limit' in employed instead of the term 'insurance sum'.

229. In the case of both these insurance types, i.e., property insurance and liability insurance, Latvian insurance contract law explicitly allows insurance contract

124. Articles 39 and 40(1) ICA.
125. Article 51(3) ICA.
126. Article 37(3) ICA.

parties to choose another procedure for establishing the amounts of insurance redress within multiple insurance,[127] provided that they cannot be contrary to the compensation principle.

230. An additional rule is envisaged for provision of insurance redress that is provided in both a voluntary and a compulsory insurance which may be covered by the term of multiple insurance as well. This situation is regulated by Article 38 ICA which provides as follows:

> If an insurance object has concurrently been insured in compulsory and voluntary insurance, the voluntary insurance compensation shall be paid irrespective of the conditions of the compulsory insurance compensation, in compliance with the provisions of Section 35 of this Law.

231. As it could be observed from this provision, Latvian insurance contract law disallows multiple insurance if insurance redress is provided both in voluntary and compulsory insurance. The reference in the commented provision to Article 35 ICA implies application of the compensation principle which would mean that the insurance contract in the case of voluntary insurance shall be fulfilled by the insurer insofar as damage is not compensated within compulsory insurance. Considering that provision of insurance redress in compulsory insurance prevails over its provision in voluntary insurance, one may arrive at conclusion that Article 38 ICA quoted above envisages dominance of compulsory insurance over voluntary insurance from the point of view of provision of insurance redress.

232. An exception from the application of regulation of multiple insurance is provided for in cases of personal insurance. Article 39 ICA envisages the duty for insurers to provide insurance redress in the case of multiple insurance in personal insurance. At the same time, this provision prescribes that this rule does not apply in 'the cases when use of the compensation principle is specified in the insurance contract'. The compensation principle cannot be applied in personal insurance as it was discussed above, therefore, this exception should not be taken into account.

§3. Subrogation

233. Subrogation is one of the possibilities for distribution of the material consequences of the insured risks within the society. The aim of subrogation is twofold. On the one hand, it allows an insurer to avoid bearing the material consequences of an insured event alone. On the other, it carries on public interest to disallow the liable person to avoid legal liability for its illegal conduct solely on the account of the insurer.

---

127. Article 37(4) ICA.

234. Latvian legal literature has discussed the issue of subrogation in respect of both general civil law regulation and specifically insurance contract law. According to authoritative opinions expressed in Latvian legal literature, the Latvian Civil Act does not recognise legal institute of subrogation.[128] At the same, insurance contract regulation is provided by special legal norms included in a separate legal act, namely the Insurance Contract Act. Considering these special legal norms, both Latvian legal literature[129] and court practice of Latvian court have admitted application of subrogation in Latvian insurance contract law. Latvian insurance contract law is familiar with general and special regulation of subrogation depending on an insurance type – both types of regulation will be discussed further in detail.

235. The general regulation of subrogation in insurance contract law is provided in Article 40 ICA, but there is a special regulation concerning motor insurance law in Article 41 of the Motor Insurance Act.[130]

236. The general regulation of subrogation in insurance law is based on the legal definition of subrogation. However, it should be taken into account that the term 'subrogation' is not used in Latvian insurance contract law, but instead the term 'recourse claim' is employed.

237. Article 40(1) ICA provides the legal definition and one limitation of subrogation:

> An insurer who has paid insurance compensation shall take over the right of claim of an insured person against a person who is responsible for loss, except the cases when harm to the life, health or physical state of a person has been caused. This exception shall not be in force if use of the compensation principle is specified in the insurance contract.

238. As one may notice from the first sentence of this paragraph of Article 40, it provides the example of statutory subrogation by referring to overtaking the right of claim by the insurer against a tortfeasor after providing the insurance redress to

128. For instance, Sinaiskis V. Latvijas civiltiesību apskats: Lietu tiesības, Saistību tiesības. Rīga: Latvijas Juristu biedrība, 1996, 119. lpp. For a detailed discussion, *see* Mantrovs V. Regresa prasības regulējums Latvijas apdrošināšanas tiesībās. Grām.: Ārvalsts investīcijas: kad tiesības mijiedarbojas: Latvijas Universitātes 74. zinātniskās konferences rakstu krājums. Rīga: LU Akadēmiskais apgāds, 2016, 413.lpp. (especially footnote 33).

129. Juridisko terminu vārdnīca. Autoru kolektīvs. Rīga: Nordik, 1998, 248. lpp.; Mantrovs V. Regresa prasības regulējums Latvijas apdrošināšanas tiesībās. Grām.: Ārvalsts investīcijas: kad tiesības mijiedarbojas: Latvijas Universitātes 74. zinātniskās konferences rakstu krājums. Rīga: LU Akadēmiskais apgāds, 2016, 413.lpp.

130. Regulation of subrogation included in this Article is discussed below in Part IV devoted to motor insurance.

the insured person. Such wording leads to the conclusion that this provision explicitly provides for subrogation by characterising its nature but not for other possibilities for overtaking the claim such as cession which is familiar to regulation of Latvian law of obligations[131].

239. Article 40 of the Insurance Contract Act provides five limitations of a subrogation right. The first sentence of Article 40(1) ICA provides the first limitation of a subrogation right by stating that it does not apply to personal insurance which is reflected in the wording 'except the cases when harm to the life, health or physical state of a person has been caused'. Though the second sentence in Article 40(1) ICA provides that this exception does not apply if the compensation principle is used in the case of personal insurance, one may assume that this rule has no effect as the compensation principle cannot be involved to assess the value of life, health and physical integrity. The other four limitations of a subrogation right are provided in other paragraphs of Article 40 ICA.

240. The second limitation is envisaged in the case if the provided insurance redress does not compensate fully the damage caused in the case of occurrence of the insured risk. Such situation may take place, for instance, in the case of deductibles (excess) frequently used in property insurance and liability insurance contracts. In this situation, the insurer may exploit its subrogation right in one of the following three cases: if the insurer or the victim abandons the claim against the tortfeasor; simultaneously bringing a claim (the priority for compensation of the damages is given to the insured or the victim and only after the damages has been paid in full, the insurer may be compensated if there are sufficient assets on the part of the tortfeasor); or expiry of the one-year term commencing from the moment of payment of insurance redress.[132]

241. The next limitation concerns the immunity of persons who are exempted from application of a subrogation right, namely, the children, parents or spouse of the insured with a subrogation action; an exception shall be such insurable events which are caused in bad faith or due to gross negligence.[133] Furthermore, this provision was criticised in Latvian legal literature due to its old-fashioned wording disregarding the nature of subrogation.[134] This provision on immunity from a subrogation claim does not take into account modern family relationships such as relationships between foster children and foster parents or partner relationships based on an unregistered marriage.[135] Likewise, this provision does not envisage that employees or persons in similar relationships, which are covered by a liability insurance contract, also enjoy immunity from a subrogation claim.[136]

---

131. Article 1793 CL et seq.
132. Article 40(2)–(5) ICA.
133. Article 40(7) ICA.
134. Regresa prasības regulējums Latvijas apdrošināšanas tiesībās, grām.: Ārvalsts investīcijas: kad tiesības mijiedarbojas: Latvijas Universitātes 74. zinātniskās konferences rakstu krājums. R.: LU Akadēmiskais apgāds, 2016, 408–419.lpp.
135. *Ibid.*
136. *Ibid.*

242. The last limitation concerns a special term of limitation period.[137] Latvian insurance contract law envisages a special term of limitation period where a subrogation right is exercised against the insured when the special term of limitation period is provided within three years from the day of payment of the insurance redress.[138] If a subrogation right is exploited by other persons, the general term of limitation period applies which is ten years.

243. A specific provision is provided in the case if the recourse claim is not possible due to bad faith or gross negligence of an insured. In this situation, the insurer may request from the insured reimbursement of the insurance redress paid in the amount by which subrogation action is not possible.[139] As it could be observed from the broad wording 'the recourse claim is not possible' included in Article 40(6) ICA, these situations may cover all possibilities for unsuccessful outcome of the recourse claim, for instance, occurrence of the insured risk with bad faith or gross negligence or failure to submit documents or provide accurate information to the insurer.

137. For a discussion of limitation period, *see* Ch. 10 of the Part II above.
138. Article 40(8) ICA.
139. Article 40(6) ICA.

Chapter 2. Property Insurance in General

244. Property insurance relates to all things that could be considered as civil law objects including lawful interests. An insurance object in property insurance is defined by Article 1 (7)(a) ICA by covering 'valuable property or interests', i.e., corporeal and non-corporeal things. Latvian insurance contract law provides special regulation for several essential issues of property insurance. These issues will be discussed separately within this chapter.

§1. Specifics of Application of the Compensation Principle

245. The specifics of property insurance are related to the special application of the compensation principle in conjuncture with the value of the insured object. This situation is different from liability insurance as an insurance object in civil liability insurance refers to civil liability of the insured and, for that reason, the value of the insured object is not involved. Rather the insurance object in civil liability insurance relates to damage caused by the insured which is expressed in the amount of damages (losses).

246. Latvian insurance contract law provides a regulation for the special application of the compensation principle directly in property insurance. In this situation, two different yet mutually related concepts are used, i.e., overinsurance and underinsurance, depending on whether the value of the insured object is above or below the insured sum. At the same time, Latvian insurance contract law does not provide a regulation for establishing the value of the insured object. In this situation, this value depends on the terms of a particular insurance contract. In practice the value of the insured object is established differently for movable things and immovable things. In the case of movables, the value of the insured thing is usually linked either with (1) the purchase fee from which a certain amount of percentage is deducted each year following the date of purchase or (2) market value. In the case of immovables, the value of the insured object is established on the basis of reinstatement value from which the rate of depreciation (i.e., wear and tear) is deducted.

247. Article 36 ICA provides regulation for overinsurance. Article 36(1) ICA envisages that in the case of overinsurance, the value of the insured object shall be reduced in chronological order of entering into contracts until this sum does not exceed that value. An exception to this rule is provided in those cases where insurance contracts are concluded in bad faith or with gross negligence of the policyholder in which cases by declaring such a contract as invalid.[140]

248. If necessary, one or several insurance contracts shall be terminated in the case of overinsurance.[141] However, the Insurance Contract Act provides that if the insured event takes place before termination of one or several insurance contracts,

140. Article 36(5) ICA.
141. Article 36(2) ICA.

the insurer has a duty to provide insurance redress in such amount corresponding to the value of the insured object.[142] Obviously, provision of insurance redress is subject to the application of the compensation principle as envisaged by Article 35 ICA. Therefore, if the amount of insurance redress exceeds the amount of damages caused to the insured person by the occurrence of the insured risk, other insurers that concluded insurance contracts shall not provide insurance redress because otherwise such insurers would act contrary to the compensation principle. Likewise, this duty upon insurers is directly provided by Article 41(1) ICA which provides that in property insurance the insurance amount may not exceed the value of an insurance object.

249. At the same time, the Insurance Contract Act allows the parties of all insurance contracts in question to agree upon other procedures to reduce the insurance amount.[143]

250. As regards underinsurance, Article 43 provides that an insurer shall pay insurance compensation in the proportion which exists between the insurance amount and its value. This provision allows derogation from this rule if it is so provided for by the insurance contract. However, insertion of such provision in an insurance contract is not usual in Latvian insurance practice.

251. Furthermore, two kinds of modifications of the compensation principle may be agreed which operate only in property insurance.

252. Article 41(2) ICA provides that parties to the insurance contract may agree upon the agreed value of an insurance object. Likewise, Article 41(3) ICA allows parties to the insurance contract to agree upon the reinstatement value of the insured object. The weakness of both provisions is in the fact that neither of the terms, i.e., agreed value or reinstatement value, are defined by the Insurance Contract Act. It leads to the situation that insurance contracts may redefine these terms by attributing to them a different meaning than that envisaged upon these provisions. For instance, in one of the court cases, Latvian courts reviewed the insurance contract which defined the term 'new value' of the insured object in the meaning of the current value of the insured object without any relation to reinstatement value. In this case, the Latvian Supreme Court revoked the judgment of the appeal instance court which clarified the term 'new value' in the meaning of the reinstatement value by disregarding the legal definition of the former term provided by the insurance contract itself.[144]

---

142. Article 36(4) ICA.
143. Article 36(3) ICA.
144. Judgment of the Latvian Supreme Court dated 10 Oct. 2007 in Case No SKC-669 [Ollis Gardums].

§2. Change of the Owner of the Insured Object

253. Another specific element of regulation of property insurance relates to the issue of change of the owner of the insured object dealt with in Article 44 ICA. This regulation depends on whether the insured object is either an immovable thing or a movable thing. In case if the insured object is an immovable thing, 'an insurance contract shall be in force in favour of the new owner, one month after all documents regarding the change of ownership rights are drawn up'.[145] Neither this nor any other provision provides possibility for insurance contract parties and the acquirer of the insured object to agree on different procedure, for instance, the continuation of the insurance contract by replacing the person who was indicated as the insured with the acquirer. This provision does not apply if the insurance contract expires or the acquirer has concluded another insurance contract before the above term.[146]

As regards movable things, an insurance contract shall terminate at the moment of transfer of the movable property to the new owner.[147] In this case, however, the Insurance Contract Act provides the possibility of an agreement on a different procedure.

§3. Other Specific Provisions

254. Latvian insurance contract law does not provide a comprehensive regulation of property insurance or regulation of different specific issues concerning property insurance (with an exception of those specific issues discussed above). However, one may still notice specific provisions concerning property insurance scattered within Latvian insurance contract regulation. Such specific provision also relates to 'especially irreplaceable object' if its is insured as the insured object. Article 42 ICA specifically concerns the situation when an 'especially irreplaceable object' considerably loses its initial value. Article 42 ICA provides that the parties to such insurance contract have the right by mutual agreement to reduce the initial value of the insured object or terminate an insurance contract. As it may be observed from the wording of Article 42 ICA, its application fully depends on an agreement of the insurance contract parties. Though this Article does not specify an insurance type which is covered by its regulation, it is clear that this provision relates to property insurance only. Likewise, this Article does not provide what the term 'especially irreplaceable object' denotes but one may arrive at a conclusion from the essence of the regulation included in Article 42 ICA that such object should have special value such as paintings, retro cars, jewellery and others.

145. Article 44(1) ICA.
146. Article 44(2) ICA.
147. Article 44(3) ICA.

§4. Fire Insurance

255. The Insurance Contract Act does not envisage specific rules concerning fire insurance. Neither are such specific rules provided from the point of view of insurance supervision in the Insurance and Reinsurance Act. Therefore, fire insurance is subject to general regulation on property insurance included in the Insurance Contract Act and specific contract terms included in a particular insurance contract.

256. Latvian insurers usually offer to cover premises (buildings, living houses, apartments, etc) against the risk of fire. Insurance of premises against fire risk usually is not offered separately, but insurance against fire risks is included among other insured risks in a particular insurance contract such as explosion risks, leakage from engineering communications, lighting risk as well as similar risks. Latvian insurers also usually define the risk of fire in a particular insurance contract.

257. Latvian courts have reviewed different court disputes involving a collection of insurance redress in the case of occurrence of fire risk; however, as far as the anonymised database of court practice of Latvian courts is concerned, the Latvian Supreme Court has not dealt so far with the understanding of fire risk from the general point of view. However, Latvian courts have analysed policyholders' or insureds' duties concerning the occurrence of fire risk. In one of the cases, Latvian courts considered whether an insurer could refuse insurance redress in fire insurance if a policyholder or an insured has failed to inform the insurer about pledging the insured house before the conclusion of insurance contract provided for such a duty. By revoking the judgment of the appeal instance court, the Latvian Supreme Court pointed out, inter alia, that it should be considered whether the failure to comply with such a duty influenced the probability of increasing the insured risk, i.e., fire risk.[148]

§5. Motor Vehicle Insurance

258. Insurance in respect of motor vehicles covers two types of insurance. One type of insurance relates to hull insurance (the so-called Casco insurance) covering motor vehicles as insured objects in property insurance (motor vehicle insurance). Another type relates to civil liability of motor vehicle drivers (the so-called motor insurance) discussed below separately in Part IV.

259. Latvian insurance contract law does not provide specific regulation for motor vehicle insurance. Therefore, motor vehicle insurance is subject to the general regulation of property insurance and to contract terms included in a particular

148. Judgment of the Latvian Supreme Court of 14 Feb. 2014 in Case No SKC-17/2014 [not reporting about pledging of a living house in fire risk insurance]. Available in Latvian at http://at.gov.lv/files/uploads/files/archive/department1/2014/SKC-17-2014.doc.

motor vehicle insurance contract. Motor vehicle insurance takes one of the most significant places in insurance structure in Latvia and occupies the third place among all insurance branches based on written insurance premiums (*bruto*).[149]

§6. Illegal Conduct Insurance

260. Similarly, as other special property insurance types discussed above, insurance against illegal conduct with respect to corporal and non-corporal things as insurance objects within property insurance is left without special regulation.

261. In Latvian insurance practice, illegal conduct is usually insured in combination with other insured risks than separately. One may refer to hull insurance, especially concerning motor vehicle insurance or insurance of immovables (apartments, living houses, different kind of premises, production buildings, factories, etc.) as usual examples of such combined insurance. Depending on insurance contract terms, insurance of an insurance object against illegal conduct may cover theft, burglary, damage made to windows or doors, etc.

§7. Legal Expense Insurance

262. Legal expense insurance relates to coverage of expenses arising from the use of legal assistance (legal services) in accordance with an insurance contract in question. Legal expense insurance is not widespread in Latvian insurance market, especially among consumers who do not usually take possibility of legal expense insurance. Latvian insurance contract law does not currently envisage special regulation of legal expense insurance except few contractual matters under insurance supervision included in the Insurance and Reinsurance Act. Therefore, contractual matters in relation to legal expense insurance are governed by general insurance contract regulation contained in the Insurance Contract Act in conjuncture with these few contractual matters regulated within insurance supervision.

263. Special regulation concerning legal expense insurance is provided by insurance supervision regulation by transposing norms of the Solvency II Directive (specifically by section 4, Chapter II, Title II of the Solvency II Directive). Specifically, Chapter XXV (Articles 191–193) of the Insurance and Reinsurance Act envisages legal expense insurance regulation from the point of view of insurance supervision.

264. Article 191 of the Insurance and Reinsurance Act concerns the scope of legal expense insurance regulation within Chapter XXV of this Act. Article 191(1) of the Insurance and Reinsurance Act envisages that this chapter covers pursuing of insurance of such legal expenses that fall within a specific insurance class on legal

149. Finanšu un kapitāla tirgus komisija [Financial and Capital Market Commission]. Pārskats par finanšu un kapitāla tirgu 2016.gadā [Overview over financial and capital market in the year of 2016]. Available in Latvian at http://www.fktk.lv/attachments/article/6203/Parskats_Q4_2016.pdf.

expense insurance whose pursuit requires a separate licence.[150] Likewise, this provision provides a legal definition of legal expense insurance by referring to legal expenses which arise during court proceedings, out-of-court procedures in criminal or administrative procedure or even outside of such procedures. At the same time, Article 191(2) of that Act makes it clear that legal expense insurance does not relate to coverage of legal expenses arising from marine insurance, civil liability insurance or assistance insurance.

265. Article 192 of the Insurance and Reinsurance Act deals with claims management within an insurance contract in legal expense insurance.

266. The first sentence of this Article makes it clear that claims management may be assigned to another competent person. Such assignment involves outsourcing services which are generally subject to requirements of Chapter VIII of this Act. However, this chapter does not provide any additional rules for claims management in general or claims management bodies.

267. The second sentence of that Article provides for limitation of activity of the employee of an insurer who deals with claims management specifically within legal expense insurance. In this situation, this employee may act only within the field of legal expense insurance and, therefore, cannot be involved in any activity in other insurance classes.

268. Article 193 of the Insurance and Reinsurance Act deals with certain contractual matters in relation to combined insurance contracts involving, inter alia, insurance of legal expenses and choice of an attorney.

269. Specifically, Article 193 (1) (1) of this Act provides for separation of legal expense insurance from insurance of other insurable risks if insurance of legal expenses is combined with insurance of other insurable risks within a single insurance contract.

270. Likewise, Article 193(1)(2) of this Act envisages that an insured has a right to choose an attorney or 'other qualified person'. Neither this nor any other provision provides the understanding of the terms 'attorney' or 'other qualified person'. However, the former term obviously refers to sworn attorneys, i.e., attorneys admitted to the Latvian Bar Association. The possibility to use 'other qualified person' instead of the sworn attorney seems problematic as there is no such person to be established under Latvian law who would have both qualification and its verification as it is in the case of a sworn attorney. At the same time, the exploitation of the right referred to in Article 193(1)(2) is not possible in the case of use of motor vehicles or assistance insurance involving motor vehicles.[151]

150. Article 19(1)(17) Insurance and Reinsurance Act.
151. Article 193(4) Insurance and Reinsurance Act.

271. In addition, other provisions contained in this Article preclude conflict of interests concerning the insured and the insurer in respect of an attorney who represents the interests of the insured.

§8. Other Types of Property Insurance

272. Other types of property insurance such as loss of benefits insurance, suretyship insurance and the like are not subject to any special rules within Latvian insurance contract law. Thus, insurance contract parties to these special property insurance contracts may take advantage of the principle of freedom of contracts while drafting insurance contract terms. At the same time, these insurance contract terms may not come in conflict with general regulation of law of obligations and general insurance contract law in respect of mandatory norms included in both regulations. Latvian insurance market is familiar with conclusion of insurance contracts concerning these special property insurance cases. However, the number of disputes in relation to such contracts remains limited in Latvian court case practice.

Chapter 3. Liability Insurance (General Liability Insurance, Professional Liability, Product Liability, Environmental Insurance, etc.)

273. Regulation of liability insurance is generally provided in Chapter VIII of the Insurance Contract Act, together with the regulation of property insurance ('insurance against losses and damages' in the terminology of the Insurance Contract Act). Therefore, liability insurance is governed both by the joint regulation covering simultaneously liability insurance and property insurance and by special legal norms, which apply to liability insurance only, contained in Chapter VIII of the Insurance Contract Act. In addition, professional liability insurance is subject to special legal norms in relation to specific persons in separate legal acts which provide either compulsory insurance or special norms concerning professional liability insurance.

274. The insurance object in liability insurance is defined as the civil liability of a person[152] and further characterised as 'insuring the civil liability of a person from the losses caused to third parties as the result of action or failure to act of a person'.[153] As insurance object in civil liability relates to damages caused within civil liability; this insurance may not cover liability arising from other types of legal liability. Therefore, Article 49(3) ICA specifically provides that insurance redress in civil liability insurance 'shall not cover a fine and other similar payments' arising from other types of legal liability such as criminal liability or administrative liability.

§1. Retroactive and Continuing Insurance

275. One of the specific issues of liability insurance refers to damage caused by the insured that took place outside of the term of an insurance contract. Two different situations may arise in this case. The first situation refers to the so-called retroactive insurance. Retroactive insurance takes place if the insured risk occurs before the liability insurance contract becomes valid, but the parties of the contract did not know about the fact of occurrence of the insured risk during conclusion of that contract. Another situation relates to continuing insurance. Continuing insurance covers damage which is caused by occurrence of the insured risk, but the claim is submitted after expiry of the term of the liability insurance contract in question. Both retroactive insurance and continuing insurance are familiar to Latvian insurance law; however, their application in a particular insurance contractual relationship depends on the terms of an insurance contract.

152. Article 1(7)(2) ICA.
153. Article 1(16) ICA.

276. Retroactive insurance is specifically regulated in Article 45 ICA with the title 'Losses Incurred Prior to Entering into an Insurance Contract'. This Article provides that:

> A civil liability insurance contract may provide for the covering of losses which have been caused by an event related to the losses through causal relationship which has occurred before the entering into force of the insurance contract, provided that neither of the parties had been aware of the occurrence thereof at the moment of entering into the contract.

277. As one may observe from this provision, it contains a dispositive norm; therefore, choice of retroactive insurance in a liability insurance contract fully depends on insurance contract parties. This Article provides for the certain requirements for retroactive insurance to take place – if the choice of retroactive insurance is made by insurance contract parties, then these requirements apply as mandatory norms.

278. As regards claims of damages after expiry of term of validity of an insurance contract, i.e., continuing insurance, they are regulated by Article 46 ICA which provides that:

> An insurer in civil liability insurance may cover the losses incurred during the term of validity of the entered into insurance contract, if the insured person with regard to the event which has caused the losses has brought an action for recovery of losses within three years after the expiry of the term of validity of the insurance contract.

279. The structure of Article 46 ICA is similar to the one included in Article 45 ICA in relation to retroactive insurance discussed above. Again, Latvian insurance contract law allows choice of this option in liability insurance, but, if such option is chosen, the insurance contract parties shall comply with the requirements set out in this provision. A specific rule is introduced in continuing insurance concerning the term for submitting a claim for provision of insurance redress which differs from retroactive insurance. As one may notice from the very wording of Article 46 ICA quoted above, losses may be compensated if a claim of the insured has been brought 'within three years after the expiry of term of validity of the insurance contract'. As this requirement is provided on the basis of mandatory legal norms, insurance contract parties are not allowed to extend or shorten this three-year period.

§2. Scope of Insurance Redress

280. Liability insurance has its own specifics also in relation to insurance contract terms as the term 'liability limit' is used instead of the term 'insurance sum'. Article 49(1) ICA reiterates that an insurer may provide insurance redress within the amount of the liability limit to the victim.[154] However, the Insurance Contract Act allows for insurance contract parties to extend coverage also to additional expenditures such as those 'related to judicial proceedings, expert-examination or other activities based on the settlement of claim' (Article 49(2) ICA).

281. A specific ground for coverage of damage caused to the insurer by an insured person in liability insurance is provided in Article 49(4) ICA. This Article states that:

> [If] bad faith or gross negligence of an insured person has been a cause for not participating in investigation activities prescribed by law or by a judicial procedure, the insured person shall reimburse to the insurer all losses incurred by this action or failure to act.

§3. Occurrence of the Insured Risk

282. Another specific issue of civil liability insurance is related to provision of insurance redress as it refers to damages caused by the insured to the victim who is not a party to a liability insurance contract. Latvian insurance contract law does not provide any specific regulation on how civil liability of the insured person and, subsequently, liability of the insurer to provide insurance redress should be established. One may assume that in the case of dispute, two court proceedings would be necessary: one for establishing civil liability, but another establishing validity of claim to provide insurance redress. However, if there is not a dispute among the insurer, the insured and the victim, the insurer may provide insurance redress to the victim in the out of court procedure.

283. Two specific rules, however, concerning negotiations with the victim concerning occurrence of the insured risk are provided: one involving the insurer, another concerning mutual negotiations between the insured person and the victim.

284. The former type of negotiations between the insurer and the victim is referred to in Article 47 ICA. Article 47(1) ICA provides that the insurer has the right to act in favour of an insured person and represent the interests of the insured However, this right is valid from the moment of bringing an action by the victim for compensation of losses against the insured. The very fact that the insurer is involved in negotiations with the victim shall not imply, as Article 47(2) ICA specifically provides, that the insurer automatically acknowledges the liability of an insured person. At the same time, the right of the insurer to engage in such negotiations is desirable as the insurer may involve in protection of the interests of the insured person (and simultaneously its own interests as well).

154. Please note that the Insurance Contract Act employs the term 'third person' in the place of the term 'victim'.

285. The latter type of negotiations between the insured and the victim is the object of a regulation under Article 48 ICA. Article 48(1) ICA provides the rule that whenever a compensation or even a promise is given by the insured person to the victim without the written consent of an insurer, this compensation or its promise shall not be binding on the insurer. At the same time, as Article 48(2) ICA states that if the insured has taken measures for reducing losses or provided emergency assistance to the injured person, the insurer shall not, therefore, have the right to waive the obligations imposed on him or her by the insurance contract.

§4. Direct Action

286. As it was discussed in the previous Part of this monograph, Latvian insurance contract law contains a general regulation of direct action in Article 50 ICA. However, application of direct action is possible, as provided by this Article, only if a special legal norm in other legal acts envisages such direct action. Motor insurance regulation is a usual example where direct action is provided. Latvian motor insurance law discussed below in Part IV is not an exception to this situation as it also provides for direct action possibility.

§5. General Liability Insurance

287. According to the general rule for compensation of damage envisaged in Article 1635(1) CL, a tortfeasor shall compensate damage caused to another person. It should be noted that there is a dispute among Latvian civil law scholars whether this provision covers just delicts (non-contractual obligations) or is to be applied to all liability grounds (i.e., arising also from contracts and pursuant to law according to Article 1402 CL). However, if the former interpretation possibility is assumed, Article 1635(1) CL would then become the general basis for establishing civil liability irrespective of a ground of occurrence of particular obligations right.

288. General civil liability insurance applies to civil liability caused outside of any professional or commercial activity. Usually it is incurred by consumers in relation to their everyday life. It is a rare situation in Latvian insurance practice that a consumer chooses to conclude a general liability insurance contract on a general basis covering all possible activities that could cause damage to a third person. Rather, this type of insurance is employed in relation to a particular insurance object. For instance, the owner (or a lawful user but it would be a rare situation) of an apartment may insure his or her civil liability in respect of damage caused to owners of other apartments in the building.

289. Latvian insurance contract law does not provide compulsory conclusion in respect of general civil liability insurance. At the same time, conclusion of such a contract may arise from another contract. For instance, if a bank issues a loan by using an immovable as security (i.e., a mortgage contract), the contract usually requires the conclusion of a property insurance contract in relation to that immovable but not conclusion of a general civil liability insurance contract in addition. At the same time, an insurer usually offers the owner of an apartment to insure his or her civil liability arising from the use of an apartment as a linked contract in addition to insurance of the apartment in property insurance.

§6. Professional Liability Insurance

290. Professional liability insurance occupies a special part in the regulation of liability insurance and relates to the insurance of civil liability arising from carrying out a particular profession or activity. Professional liability insurance may cover any type of damages either directly or indirectly caused within the course of a particular professional activity. Regulation of professional liability insurance is not provided by general insurance contract law but is scattered among separate legal acts in relation to either a particular profession or activity.

291. Specifically, these separate legal acts usually provide a regulation of professional liability insurance only if it is a part of compulsory insurance.

292. An exception to this regulation of professional liability insurance is provided to sworn attorneys in whose case compulsory insurance is not envisaged. However, if a sworn attorney has not insured his or her professional liability concerning legal assistance provided then he or she must inform the client about the fact of non-insurance of his or her professional liability (Article 114 of the Advocacy Act of the Republic of Latvia).

§7. Product Liability Insurance

293. Product liability insurance covers civil liability of a producer related to deficiencies arising from the manufacture of goods (products). Product liability is indirectly regulated in the Latvian Civil Act but directly in separate legal acts. As regards the Latvian Civil Act, it applies to defects of alienated goods but only if a contract is concluded with a producer itself. However, separate legal acts provide product liability regulation in conjuncture with EU directives. In this regard, the Safety of Goods and Services Act[155] concerning product liability which is based on norms of EU directives on product liability[156] should be mentioned as well as the

155. Law on the Safety of Goods and Services. The official translation into English is available on the official web page of the Terminology and Translation Centre at http://www.vvc.gov.lv/export/sites/default/docs/LRTA/Likumi/Law_on_the_Safety_of_Goods_and_Services.pdf.

156. Council Directive 87/357/EEC of 25 Jun. 1987 on the approximation of the laws of the Member States concerning products which, appearing to be other than they are, endanger the health or safety of consumers; Directive 2001/95/EC of the European Parliament and of the Council of 3 Dec. 2001 on general product safety.

Liability for Defective Goods and Deficient Services Act[157] which transposes the Directive on liability for defective products[158] concerning damage caused by unsafe products or services. This legal regime is based on strict liability and in such a qualification it is discussed in Latvian legal literature.[159]

294. Latvian insurance contract law does not provide that product liability insurance is subject to compulsory insurance. Therefore, the conclusion of a product liability insurance contract depends on the risk awareness of each particular producer. It was not possible for the author of these lines to find any official statistics on the use of product liability insurance in Latvian insurance practice; however, it could be assumed that a producer might be willing to conclude a product liability insurance.

295. Product liability insurance is not subject to any specific regulation in Latvian insurance contract law. Thus, a product liability insurance contract is subject to general regulation of insurance contract law included in the Insurance Contract Act.

§8. Environmental Insurance

296. Damage caused to environment is treated as a delict (non-contractual obligation) within the meaning of Article 1635 CL and shall be compensated on the basis of strict liability. The principle of strict liability for establishing civil liability in the case of damage caused to environment is anchored in the principle 'Polluter Pays' which is provided for in Article 3(1)(1) of the Environmental Protection Act[160] and used for compensation of damage caused to environment.

297. Environmental insurance usually is included in professional or general civil liability insurance if a particular activity could lead to damage caused to environment. Separate insurance types also include environmental insurance or insurance of damage caused to environment. A motor insurance is an example of this situation. The Motor Insurance Act provides that damage to environment is also covered by the insured risks within a motor insurance contract. In this regard, the Motor Insurance Act states that a loss caused to the property of a third person in a road

157. Law on Liability for Defective Goods and Deficient Services. The official translation into English is available on the official web page of the Terminology and Translation Centre at http://www.vvc.gov.lv/export/sites/default/docs/LRTA/Likumi/On_Liability_for_Defective_Goods_and_Deficient_Services.doc.
158. Council Directive 85/374/EEC of 25 Jul. 1985 on the approximation of the laws, regulations and administrative provisions of the Member States concerning liability for defective products.
159. Torgāns K. Saistību tiesības. Mācību grāmata. R.: Tiesu namu aģentūra, 2014, 190–194.lpp.; Torgāns K. Līgumu un deliktu tiesību problēmas. R.: Tiesu namu aģentūra, 2013, 248–264.lpp.
160. Environmental Protection Law. The official translation into English is available on the official web page of the Terminology and Translation Centre at http://www.vvc.gov.lv/export/sites/default/docs/LRTA/Likumi/Environmental_Protection_Law.doc.

traffic accident is a loss that has arisen, inter alia, 'due to the damage to the environment'.[161] Furthermore, Article 30 MIA prescribes types of losses due to damage to environment to be compensated by the insurer, including 'expenses for the determination, confinement and minimisation of the damage, the collection, neutralisation or elimination, or processing, of pollution, the removal of the damaged topsoil, neutralisation or elimination thereof and replacement with a new topsoil'.

161. Article 25(1)(7) Motor Insurance Act.

Chapter 4. Other Specific Types of Insurance

298. There are such specific insurance types which are not frequently used in Latvian insurance practice because of the size of Latvian insurance market, insurance demand in Latvian insurance market and lack of specific regulation for these specific insurance types. Therefore, one may hardly speak in Latvian insurance market from regulation point of view concerning such special insurance types as aviation and space insurance (except compulsory insurance of aircrafts[162]), agricultural insurance, hail insurance, livestock insurance, catastrophe insurance including nuclear risks and natural catastrophes, credit and caution insurance or technical insurance.

299. It should be mentioned that insurance supervision regulation transposes norms of the Solvency II Directive in relation to specific insurance types such as assistance insurance[163] or legal expense insurance.[164] However, neither this Act nor the Insurance Contract Act provides any specific regulation concerning contractual issues in respect of an insurance contract to be concluded within any of these insurance types.

162. For a discussion of compulsory insurance, *see* General Introduction above.
163. Chapter XXIV Insurance and Reinsurance Act.
164. Chapter XXV Insurance and Reinsurance Act.

Part IV. Motor Insurance

Chapter 1. General Overview

300. Latvian insurance contract law treats motor insurance as a specific insurance type and provides its regulation in a separate legal act, i.e., the Motor Insurance Act. The specifics of regulation of motor insurance in Latvia relate to exhaustive regulation of motor insurance at the legislative level. The Motor Insurance Act provides comprehensive and exhaustive regulation of a motor insurance contract. Therefore, one may rightly conclude that a motor insurance contract is regulated entirely on the legislative level leaving motor insurance contract parties with the sole choice of the type of a motor insurance contract, its term and the amount of insurance premium. At the same time, separate non-regulated aspects are governed either by general insurance contract law such as general regulation of recourse claim or by general law of obligations such as contractual issues.

301. The above approach for regulation of a motor insurance contract at the legislative level chosen by the Latvian legislator has a twofold impact.

302. One the one hand, it limits the exercise of the principle of freedom of contract by insurance contract parties by disallowing them to individualise contract terms for each particular motor insurance contract type, motor vehicle, owner of a motor vehicle, motor vehicle driver, etc.

303. On the other, such approach produces specific results. For instance, as regulation of motor insurance contracts is based on statutory regulation, it cannot be subject to protection of policyholders being consumers on the basis of unfair or ambiguous standard contract terms. This exception is not provided by the Consumer Rights Protection Act, yet it is explicitly envisaged by the Unfair Terms Directive. Thus, if any provision included in the Motor Insurance Contract Act is contrary to regulation of unfair standard contract terms, such a term may be disputed only at the Constitutional Court.

304. In addition to regulation provided by the Motor Insurance Act, certain motor insurance law aspects are envisaged by other legal acts. A specific role is attributed to two regulatory enactments of the Cabinet concerning the quantification of damage caused in a road traffic accident. One of these regulatory enactments covers pecuniary (material) damage caused to a person but another – non-pecuniary (non-material) damage caused to a person.

Likewise, different documents adopted by the Latvian national insurers' bureau may be applied by a Latvian motor insurer in relation to calculation of amounts of insurance premiums, damages, etc. Latvian courts have admitted that these documents may be applied by Latvian courts in the case of dispute; however, they are not binding on Latvian courts.

Chapter 2. Types of Motor Insurance Contracts

305. The Motor Insurance Act distinguishes three types of motor insurance contracts and lays down rules for their conclusion and termination, i.e., a standard contract, a frontier insurance contract and the international insurance contract (which is simultaneously covered by the term 'Green Card') (Article 4 MIA).

306. The *standard contract* is one of the motor insurance contract types that is concluded in relation to certain types of motor vehicles, i.e., motor vehicles that are registered or alienated in the territory of Latvia; motor vehicles which are alienated or registered in another country for the purpose of exporting it from that country and registering it in Latvia; and motor vehicles that are not registered in Latvia but intended for transportation of other motor vehicles (Article 5(1) MIA). The standard contract is in force in the whole territory of EEZ (Article 5(3) MIA) and can be concluded either in person or by distance means (Article 4.[1](1) MIA). The standard contract may be concluded for certain fixed periods already predefined by law such as 3, 6, 9 or 12 months with exceptions in specific situations regulated by Article 9(1) MIA.

307. The *frontier insurance contract* is concluded in relation to motor vehicles that are not registered in EEZ countries (Article 6(1)), and it is in force in the whole territory of EEZ countries (Article 6(2) MIA). This type of a motor insurance contract may be concluded only in person (Article 4.[1](2) MIA). The frontier insurance contract may be concluded within the predefined minimum and maximum term without fixed time limits: from the term of one month to twelve months (Article 9(2) MIA).

The *international insurance contract* is concluded in relation to motor vehicles registered in Latvia and participates in road traffic in a country, which is a Member State of the Green Card system (Article 7(1) MIA). The international insurance contract is in force in those Green Card system Member States which are indicated in the contract itself (Article 7(2) MIA). Likewise, the international insurance contract may be concluded only with the insurer who is a member of a Latvian national insurers' bureau (Article 7(3) MIA). Similar to the frontier insurance contract discussed in the previous paragraph, the international insurance contract may be concluded only in person (Article 4.[1](2) MIA). Likewise, as in the case of the frontier insurance contract, the international insurance contract may be concluded within the predefined minimum and maximum term without fixed time limits: from the term of fifteen days (but not one month as provided in the case of frontier insurance contract mentioned in the previous paragraph) to twelve months (Article 9(3) MIA).

Chapter 3. Duty to Conclude a Motor Insurance Contract

308. Latvian motor insurance law provides compulsory conclusion of a motor insurance contract by following EU motor insurance law.[165] Such rule explicitly arises from Article 3(2) MIA envisaging the duty of '[e]ach owner of a motor vehicle' to 'insure the civil liability'.

309. The duty to conclude the motor insurance contract is upon every owner of each motor vehicle (Article 3(2) first sentence MIA). This provision relates to the terms 'motor vehicle' and 'motor vehicle owner', both of whom are defined in the Motor Insurance Act itself. The term 'motor vehicle' is defined in Article 1(12) MIA as referring to two kinds of vehicles, namely:

(a) a road motor vehicle, a trailer (a semi-trailer), a moped that is to be registered with the Road Traffic Safety Directorate or the State Technical Supervision Agency, or with a local government or which has been registered in a foreign state,
(b) a tram that is to be registered with a local government.

310. As it could be observed from this provision, it broadens the scope of the term 'vehicle' as defined under EU motor insurance law[166] by extending this term also to trams as all vehicles on rails are excluded from the term 'vehicle' under EU motor insurance law.

311. Likewise, the Motor Insurance Act defines the owner of a motor vehicle as 'a natural or legal person who owns a motor vehicle or in whose name the motor vehicle is registered' (Article 1(13) MIA). The Latvian Supreme Court has interpreted this provision in such a way that the owner may be either a person who is registered as an owner in the motor vehicles and their drivers' register or a person who is not registered but may prove ownership rights.[167]

312. At the same time, the Motor Insurance Act extends the duty to conclude the motor insurance contract also to the lawful users of a motor vehicle if that contract is either not concluded by the owner or expired (Article 3(2) second sentence MIA). The term 'lawful user' is defined in Article 1(14) MIA as:

> [A] natural or legal person who is not the owner of a motor vehicle, but who uses the motor vehicle in road traffic on the basis of a power of attorney, rental agreement or other legal grounds.

165. Article 3(1) Codifying Motor Insurance Directive.
166. Article 1(1) Codifying Motor Insurance Directive.
167. Mantrovs V. ar Augstākās tiesas Judikatūras un zinātniski analītiskās nodaļas informatīvo atbalstu. Augstākās tiesas Civillietu departamenta prakse sauszemes transportlīdzekļu vadītāju civiltiesiskās atbildības obligātās apdrošināšanas (OCTA) lietās. R., 2015. Available in Latvian at www.at-.gov.lv.

313. From the duty to conclude the motor insurance contract is excluded such a lawful user of the motor vehicle 'who is in employment legal or service relations does not have the insurance obligation' (Article 3(2) third sentence MIA).

314. Certain essential elements of a motor insurance contract, such as the insurance object and the liability limit, are subject to the special regulation in the Motor Insurance Act to be discussed in the next Chapter of this monograph.

Chapter 4. Essential Elements

§1. Insurance Object

315. Insurance object in motor insurance is subject to special regulation provided in Article 3(1) MIA. This provision provides as follows:

> The object of a compulsory insurance shall be the civil liability of the owner or legal user of a motor vehicle (hereinafter – civil liability of an owner) for losses caused to a third person in a road traffic accident.

316. At first, it should be mentioned that, by mistake, the Motor Insurance Act defines insurance object in relation to motor vehicle owners or lawful users instead of motor vehicle drivers as provided by EU motor insurance law. Latvian courts have not paid attention to that discrepancy, but in the case of dispute this provision shall be interpreted as relating to civil liability insurance of motor vehicle drivers.

317. The term 'motor vehicle' whose driver is insured within motor insurance referred to in this provision is based on the specific understanding of that term discussed above.

Civil liability covered relates to damage caused to third parties (i.e., victims) in the result of a road traffic accident. The term 'road traffic accident' is not defined in the Motor Insurance Act but in a legal act governing road traffic, i.e., the Road Traffic Act[168]. Article 1(7) of the Road Traffic Act provides the legal definition of the term 'road traffic accident':

> an accident that has occurred in road traffic which involves at least one vehicle and as a result of which an individual has died, he or she has been caused physical injury, or damage to the property of a legal or natural person or to the environment has been caused, as well as when an accident has occurred in some other place, where driving with a vehicle is possible, and which involves a vehicle.

This provision shall be interpreted in the light of the insurance object within motor insurance as provided by Article 3(1) of the Codifying Motor Insurance Directive referring to the wording 'the use of vehicles'.

168. Road Traffic Law. The official translation into English is available on the official web page of the Terminology and Translation Centre at http://vvc.gov.lv/image/catalog/dokumenti/Road_Traffic_Law.doc.

§2. Liability Limit

318. Specific regulation of liability limit in motor insurance is provided in Article 15 MIA which strictly keeps to the liability amounts as provided by EU motor insurance law.[169] Article 15(1) MIA provides the following liability limits:

(1) for indemnification of personal losses – up to EUR 5,000,000, regardless of the number of injured persons;
(2) for indemnification of property loss – up to EUR 1,000,000, regardless of the number of third parties.

319. Article 15(2) MIA refers to the situation when damage is covered within liability limits envisaged by Article 15(1) MIA, discussed in the previous paragraph of this monograph, but this damage is not compensated fully. In this situation, Article 15(2) MIA provides that a third person is entitled to request damage, which was not compensated by the insurer, 'in accordance with the procedures laid down in laws and regulations'. This expression means that uncompensated damage may be collected if the victim brings a claim against a liable motor vehicle driver in a court of general jurisdiction on the basis of general regulation of civil liability rules.

Clarification of both above terms, i.e., insurance object and liability limit, is further provided by Chapter III of the Motor Insurance Act and is discussed in the next sub-chapter.

§3. The Risks Insured

320. Regulation of the insured risks within the motor insurance contract is provided at the level of EU motor insurance law transposed at the national level in the Motor Insurance Act.

321. As one may conclude from the regulation of the liability limit within a motor insurance contract, which is provided in Article 15(1) MIA and discussed above, two risks are insured, namely, personal losses and property losses. The meaning of both insured risks is not identical if compared with the understanding of the insured risks under EU motor insurance law. Indeed, Article 9(1) MIA provides that there are two risks, namely, personal injury and damage to property. As EU motor insurance law was interpreted by the CJEU, the former relates to non-pecuniary (non-material) damage, but the latter to pecuniary (non-material) damage.[170] The understanding of personal losses covers damage in relation to person himself or herself, i.e., damage made to the person directly, but not to movables or immovables owned by this person which are covered by another term, namely property losses. Similarly, the former term includes both material damage caused to the victim such as unearned profit or treatment expenses and non-material referring to pain and sufferings caused in the result of the motor traffic accident.

169. Article 9(1) Codifying Motor Insurance Directive.
170. Joined cases C-22/12 and C-277/12.

322. Article 19 (1) and (2) MIA provides that there are two types of personal losses, i.e., material losses and non-material losses caused to a person. The former type of losses encompasses the following losses as defined by Article 19(1) MIA, i.e.:

(1) medical treatment;
(2) temporary incapacity for employment;
(3) loss of ability to work;
(4) death.

323. Article 19(2) IMA describes what kind of damage is covered by the term 'non-material losses caused to a person in a road accident' that involve pain and mental suffering due to:

(1) a physical trauma of the injured person;
(2) the crippling or disablement of the injured person;
(3) the death of a breadwinner, dependant or spouse;
(4) Group I disability of a breadwinner, dependant or spouse.

The amount of insurance redress and its calculation is further provided by two regulations of the Cabinet (Article 19(3) MIA) discussed below.

324. A detailed regulation concerning types of damage covered by material loss caused to a person and referred to in Article 19(1) MIA is subject to further regulation in Articles 20–23 MIA. In addition, inflation percentage shall be applied in the case of calculation of losses in the result of loss of ability to work or death. At the same time, if these losses are covered from either a state or municipal budget, an insurer or a Latvian national insurers' bureau shall compensate these expenses to these institutions on the basis of Article 24 MIA.

325. At the same time, quantification of the amount of damage is provided by two regulatory enactments of the Cabinet (Article 19(3) MIA). One regulatory enactment concerns qualification of pecuniary (material) damage caused to a person in the result of a road traffic accident which is of technical character. Another regulatory enactment of the Cabinet deals with quantification of the amount of non-pecuniary (non-material) damage caused to a person due to a road traffic accident. For this quantification, these regulations contain methods for calculation of the amount of insurance redress. These methods are partially based on calculation of (1) certain sums; for instance, in the case of non-pecuniary damage caused to the next kin of a victim of a road traffic accident, or (2) criteria for establishing non-pecuniary damage for bodily injuries.

326. The previously effective regulatory enactment for calculation of non-pecuniary damage was partially admitted as unconstitutional due to non-compliance with EU motor insurance law after the famous *Vitalijs Drozdovs* case[171] insofar as they establish fixed amounts of compensation for non-pecuniary damage.[172] The effective regulatory enactment contains the similar approach as the previously effective regulatory enactment with minor difference: the current approach is based on fixed amounts of insurance redress expressed in a certain number of minimum wages but the previous approach referred to certain amounts of insurance redress. The currently effective regulatory enactment is already criticised in Latvian legal literature considering its possible unconstitutional character.[173]

327. At the same time, another insured risk, i.e., property losses, is regulated on the basis of Articles 25–30 MIA. The understanding of the term 'a loss caused to the property of a third person in a road traffic accident' is characterised by the list of types of losses covered by that term in Article 25(1) MIA and is as follows:

(1) due to the damage or total loss of a motor vehicle;
(2) due to the damage or total loss of a road, a road construction, a building or a structure;
(3) due to the damage or total loss of another property owned by the person, except the property referred to in paragraph 1, Clauses 1 and 2 of this Section;
(4) while carrying out the rescue operations of persons who have suffered in a road traffic accident;
(5) due to the damage of a motor vehicle used for the transportation of the injured person to a medical treatment institution or the soiling of the interior of such motor vehicle;
(6) while removing motor vehicles from the site of the road traffic accident;
(7) due to the damage to the environment.

328. Further Articles 26–30 IMA characterise what kind of damage is understood under each type of loss caused to the property of a third person in a road traffic accident.

171. CJEU Case C-277/12 *Vitālijs Drozdovs v. Baltikums AAS* (ECLI:EU:C:2013:685). For a discussion of this case, *see* Mantrov V. Is 142 Euro Equal to 350 000 Euro? The CJEU Interpretation of 'Personal Injury' and 'Injured Party' in EU Motor Insurance Law. *European Journal of Risk Regulation*, 2014, pp. 399–406.
172. Judgement of the Constitutional Court dated 29 Dec. 2014 in the Case No Nr.2014-06-03.
173. Mantrov V. EST tiesu prakse nemantiskā kaitējuma atlīdzināšanai OCTA ietvaros: Latvijas problēmjautājumi. Jurisprudence un kultūra: pagātnes mācības un nākotnes izaicinājumi: Latvijas Universitātes 5. starptautiskā zinātniskā konference, veltīta Latvijas Universitātes Juridiskās fakultātes 95. gadadienai, 2014. gada 10–11. novembris (Rīga, LU Akadēmiskais apgāds, 2014), 560–568.lpp.

§4. Insurance Premium

329. Despite the fact that regulation of insurance premium is contained by general regulation of insurance contract law envisaged by the ICA and general supervision regulation envisaged by the Insurance and Reinsurance Act, the MIA contains special regulation on insurance premiums to be paid under a motor insurance contract. This regulation is particularly contained in Articles 12–14 MIA as well as in other norms of the MIA in respect of specific situations, for instance, concerning repayment of the insurance premium (Article 10(5) and (6.[1]) MIA) or concerning a separate ground for a recourse claim (Article 41(2)(a) MIA).

330. Regulation included in Articles 12–14 MIA partially overlaps, especially in the case of Article 12 MIA and Article 14(1) and (6) MIA, with general regulation of insurance premium referred to in the previous paragraph. At the same time, additional rules could be identified.

Indeed, Article 13(1) MIA provides that the amount of insurance premium shall be established on the basis of previous insurance history of a particular motor vehicle owner, including the number of cases when insurance indemnity was provided; the number of administrative or criminal offences; and other factors. In addition, Article 13(2) MIA provides that a lessee shall be considered as equal to the owner of a motor vehicle for the purpose of determining the amount of an insurance premium. Similarly, as the lessee usually is a leasing company in whose name different motor vehicles are registered, the amount of insurance premium for insurance of motor vehicles being in ownership of lessees usually is higher than in the case of other motor vehicle owners.

Furthermore, Article 14(2) and (3) MIA provides special cases when reduction of insurance premium is envisaged, and this difference shall be compensated from the Guarantee fund (Article 14(4) MIA).

Finally, Article 14(5) MIA provides an exception from the real contract model envisaged for an insurance contract by general insurance contract regulation contained by the Insurance Contract Act. Indeed, this provision states that an insurance contract shall not become void if the owner of a motor vehicle has not paid insurance premium within the time period determined in the contract. However, the MIA provides in this situation that the insurer is entitled to bring a recourse claim against an owner who has not paid insurance premium fully on the basis of Article 41(2)(a) MIA (further discussed in Chapter 7 of Part IV of this monograph).

Chapter 5. Formation, Entry into Force and Termination of the Motor Insurance Contract

331. The Motor Insurance Act provides special rules concerning formation, entry into force and termination of the motor insurance contract replacing general regulation of insurance contract law in respect of these issues.

332. Formation of the motor insurance is subject to several special legal norms included in the Motor Insurance Act. Article $9.^{1}$ MIA provides certain information that should be communicated to the insurer by the policyholder, namely information about the policyholder, the insured and the particular motor vehicle. Article $9.^{1}$ (3) MIA provides liability for the policyholder for truthfulness of its communicated information about 'the assessment of the possibility of occurrence of the insured risk' which in essence resembles the regulation of a similar situation in general insurance contract law (Article 5(1) ICA).

333. After conclusion of a motor insurance contract, the motor insurer is under the duty to issue the insurance policy. In the case of a frontier insurance contract or the international insurance contract, the insurance policy shall be issued immediately after conclusion of any of these types of a motor insurance contract, whereas in the case of a standard contract, it should be issued after the request of the owner of the motor vehicle or the policyholder (Article 8(1) MIA). The Motor Insurance Act provides that the insurer is obliged to issue a duplicate of the insurance policy upon the request of the owner of the motor vehicle driver, and the fee in this case shall not exceed 2% of the amount of the insurance premium (Article 8(3) MIA).

334. It should be noted that, despite the above-mentioned duty of the insurer to issue the insurance policy, the Motor Insurance Act (similar to general insurance contract regulation included in the Insurance Contract Act) does not provide the written form requirement for the motor insurance contract to enter into force. This conclusion is testified by the provision included in Article 8(2) MIA which provides that the non-existence of a written insurance policy shall not affect the validity of the insurance contract.

335. The Motor Insurance Act may *enter into force* in any of two alternative situations explicitly provided by Article 9(4) first sentence MIA: either (1) in the moment of conclusion of the motor insurance or (2) in the moment specified in the motor insurance contract itself. At the same time, the Motor Insurance Act mandatorily provides for the last date of validity of the motor insurance contract depending on whether the motor insurance contract was concluded before, at or later than 12 AM. Second sentence of Article 9(4) MIA provides in this connection that:

> [I]f the contract enters into effect until 12AM, then, in calculating the expiry term of the contract, the day of entry of the contract into effect shall be included, but if the contract has been entered at 12AM or later, that day shall not be included.

336. The motor insurance contract *terminates* either by expiry of the term for which it is concluded (however, it is not explicitly provided by the Motor Insurance Act itself) or before that term. The latter situation is explicitly regulated in the Motor Insurance Act whose regulation contains exhaustive list of such cases in its Article 10. Article 10(1) and (2) MIA provides the following cases when the motor insurance contract terminates prematurely:

(1) the motor vehicle is alienated;
(2) the motor vehicle has left the possession of the owner, keeper or user not because of their fault, but due to illegal activities of another person and it has been notified to the relevant law enforcement authorities in accordance with the procedures laid down in laws and regulations;
(3) there is a mistake in the information indicated in the insurance contract;
(4) a legal person is liquidated or the name thereof is changed; or
(5) a motor vehicle will not be used in road traffic.

337. In any of the above cases, the policyholder is entitled to claim insurance premium for the unused insurance coverage term (Article 10(5) and ($6.^1$) MIA).

Special regulation applies in respect of termination of a motor insurance contract in the case of alienation of the motor vehicle. This case for a termination of the contract may take place either at the moment when the alienation contract is concluded (such as a donation contract, a purchase contract, a barter contract or a maintenance contract according to the understanding of these contracts in the Latvian Civil Act) or the motor vehicle is re-registered (Article 10(6) MIA).

Chapter 6. Procedure for Submitting a Claim and Its Assessment by the Insurer or the Latvian National Insurers' Bureau

338. The Motor Insurance Act provides detailed procedural rules when the victim may apply either to the insurer or the Latvian national insurers' bureau with the claim for compensation of damage caused in the result of a road traffic accident. This procedure is generally provided by Article 31 and related Articles of the Motor Insurance Act.

339. According to the general rule, the claim shall be submitted to the insurer who has concluded the motor insurance contract for civil liability insurance of a liable motor vehicle driver. An exception applies in the case of the so-called direct loss regulation when the motor vehicle driver who is the victim in a road traffic accident may apply to its own insurer who is authorised to compensate damages caused to him or her (Articles 1(10.^{1}) and 38.^{1} MIA).

340. Another general rule under the Motor Insurance Act relates to the fact that the insurer shall carry our assessment of damages caused by establishing civil liability of persons involved in the road traffic accident, including joint civil liability if any. Afterwards, the insurer shall adopt a decision concerning this claim either accepting it fully or partially or refusing it. The insurer or the Latvian national insurers' bureau shall adopt the decision on payment of insurance redress within three months from the day of receipt of the written application of the victim but not later than within one month after all of the necessary documents have been received and shall send to the victim appropriate written information (Article 39(1) MIA).

341. If the insurer or the Latvian national insurers' bureau does not comply with that term, they shall pay statutory interest in the amount of 0.1% per day (Article 39(3) MIA). This provision is important because, in accordance with settled court practice of the Latvian Supreme Court, as discussed before, statutory interest rate shall not be paid for late payment of insurance redress or ungrounded refusal to provide payment of insurance redress on the basis of general insurance contract law.[174]

342. The Motor Insurance Act provides the list of grounds for refusal of insurance redress which is exhaustive (*numerus clausus*). This list consists of fourteen insurance redress refusals included in Article 35 MIA:

An insurer or the Motor Insurers' Bureau shall not compensate:

1) losses that have arisen while using a motor vehicle but for causing which no liability results in accordance with Section 2347 of The Civil Law. These represent losses that have been caused to a third person due to *force majeure*, with the intent of the person himself or herself, or due to his or her gross negligence;

174. For a discussion of statutory interest in the case of late payment in Latvian insurance law, *see* Ch. 7 of the Part II above.

2) losses that have been caused by an unidentified motor vehicle, except the losses caused to a person referred to in Section 19 and the losses caused to property referred to in Section 25, Paragraph one, Clauses four and five of this Law. If severe bodily injuries or moderately severe bodily injuries have been caused to at least one injured person in the road traffic accident, the losses referred to in Section 25 of this Law shall be compensated to all the persons involved in the road traffic accident;
3) losses that have been caused to property of the owner or legal user of the motor vehicle that caused a road traffic accident, and personal losses caused to the driver of the motor vehicle that caused a road traffic accident. The losses referred to in this Clause shall be compensated in the cases referred to in Section 31, Paragraphs five and seven of this Law;
4) losses due to the damage, total loss or disappearance of a motor vehicle and property contained therein, if the referred to losses have been suffered by persons after a road traffic accident;
5) losses that have been caused while using a motor vehicle in a test drive or as result of use of a vehicle for a test drive or in a car race;
6) losses due to a damage of a motor vehicle or trailer hitched or otherwise attached to the motor vehicle that caused the loss in a road traffic accident;
7) losses that have been directly or indirectly caused or facilitated by ionising radiation, radioactive contamination generated by any nuclear fuel, or by a radioactive, toxic, explosive or otherwise dangerous feature of any explosive nuclear compound or nuclear component thereof;
8) non-received profit due to a road traffic accident;
9) losses that have been caused by a rock or another object that a motor vehicle or a device attached thereto has moved;
10) the expenses of an insurance company that have been incurred due to the setting in of an insurable event provided for in a health insurance contract, except the cases where, in accordance with the health insurance contract, the insurance company compensates the losses by using the principle of compensation;
11) losses that have been caused to the property of a third person, which the owner or legal user of a motor vehicle that caused a road traffic accident has accepted for commercial carriage;
12) losses due to damage or total loss of property that have been caused in such road traffic accident which should have been reported to the State Police in accordance with the laws and regulations but which has not been reported in bad faith or due to gross negligence of the persons involved in the road traffic accident;
13) losses that have arisen in the [manoeuvring] area of an airfield in a road traffic accident in which a motor vehicle and an aircraft are involved;
14) the losses caused to the property of a lessee and to the motor vehicles used in accordance with the lease agreement, which have arisen in a road traffic accident in which such motor vehicles are involved which have been leased out to one and the same lessee identified as the holder of the motor vehicles with the State Register of Vehicles and Drivers of the

Road Traffic Safety Directorate or with the information system for the tractor-type machinery and drivers thereof of the State Technical Supervision Agency.

343. The Motor Insurance Act provides for *special terms of limitation period* for submitting the claim for provision of insurance redress separately for two kinds of damages, i.e., damage to property and damage to health. In this regard, Article 38 (3) MIA provides regulation for the limitation period in the case of damage to property which would be useful to be quoted in full:

> The right of a person who claims to receive insurance indemnity for the loss caused to the property of such person to raise a claim against the insurer or the Motor Insurers' Bureau shall cease if such right has not been claimed within a period of one year from the setting in of an insurable event.

344. As it could be observed from this provision, the special term of limitation period for the loss caused to the property is provided within one year from the moment of occurrence of a road traffic accident.

345. At the same time, Article 38 (4) MIA provides a regulation for the limitation period in the case of damage to health which also would be purposeful to cite in full:

> The right of a person who claims to receive insurance indemnity for the damage caused to health to raise a claim against the insurer or Motor Insurers' Bureau shall crease if such right has not been claimed within three years from the setting in of an insurable event.

As it can be noticed, the former limitation period applies to the whole area of damage of property loss in the meaning of Articles 15(1)(2) and 25 MIA. However, the latter limitation period, only to damage to health but not to the whole area of personal losses in the meaning of Articles 15(1)(1) and 19 MIA. Therefore, this special term of limitation period does not apply concerning personal losses except damage to health which is subject, therefore, to regulation of limitation period in respect of civil liability insurance (Article 32 ICA as discussed above).

Chapter 7. Recourse Claim (Subrogation)

346. In addition to general regulation of recourse claim in the Insurance Contract Act, the Motor Insurance Act provides special legal norms concerning grounds for recourse claim within motor insurance law. Article 41 MIA is the leading and single Article for this situation. The list of recourse claim grounds contained in Article 41 MIA is exclusive and can be neither broadened nor narrowed. Likewise, the list of claimants that could bring a recourse claim and the list of defendants who may face such a recourse claim on the basis of this list of recourse claim grounds is also provided, and both these lists are exhaustive as well.

347. Article 41(1) MIA provides recourse claim grounds that could be used by an insurer regarding the following persons:

- a liable motor vehicle driver (Article 41(1) (1) MIA);
- the owner or the lessee of the motor vehicle driver in case if it was driven by the liable motor vehicle driver (Article 41(1) (2) MIA);
- the owner (manager) of the road (Article 41(1) (3) MIA);
- a person who has caused the loss in bad faith (Article 41(1) (4) MIA);
- and, finally, against a merchant, if it allowed motor vehicles intended for sale participate in road traffic contrary to provisions of the Motor Insurance Contract (i.e., Article 5(1) (3) MIA).

348. Article 41(2) MIA provides recourse claim grounds that could be used by the Latvian national insurers' bureau regarding different persons, yet the most important and frequently used recourse claim grounds (especially the first one) are indicated in Articles 41(2)(1) and 41(2)(2) MIA. These provisions provide a recourse claim right against the owner, the lessee or the lawful user of a motor vehicle if the motor insurance contract was failed to be concluded (i.e., an uninsured motor vehicle driver that caused damage in the result of the road traffic accident) or the liable driver of a motor vehicle if he or she has acquired the motor vehicle through illegal acts.

Part V. Personal Insurance (Insurance of the Person)

349. Personal insurance is traditionally recognised as one of the types of insurance (by using one of the insurance classifications based on insurable object) in addition to property insurance and civil liability insurance. Personal insurance market in Latvia is rather highly demanded and can be characterised as evolving. Personal insurance contracts are frequently concluded in respect of private health insurance in the case of employees' health insurance and life insurance.

350. Regulation of personal insurance is included in legal definitions of insurance contract law terms defined in Article 1 (insurable object, insured, beneficiary, personal insurance, gratuities (bonuses) and repurchase amount) and the last Chapter (VIII) of the Insurance Contract Act (Articles 51–55 ICA). Chapter VIII of the Insurance Contract Act does not provide comprehensive regulation on personal insurance. Rather regulation included in that Chapter is fragmentary and relates to separate issues such as the application of the insurance of fixed sums instead of the compensation principle, beneficiary and certain other specific issues of a personal insurance contract. In addition, specific rules for separate personal insurance types such as life insurance and health insurance are provided. Likewise, special legal norms such as the term of right of withdrawal in the case of a life insurance contract concluded by distance means are provided within consumer protection law.

351. As personal insurance is based on the insurance of fixed sums, a beneficiary in question shall be entitled to receive compensation of non-pecuniary (non-material) damage from different sources. This principle is provided explicitly by Article 52 ICA which provides that payments which an insured person or beneficiary has received from other sources shall not reduce obligations of the insurer unless parties to the insurance contract have otherwise agreed in the insurance contract.

352. Article 53(1) ICA provides that a policyholder is entitled to appoint one or several beneficiaries in life and accident insurance as well as to replace them at any time during the operational time of the insurance contract.

353. A specific provision included in Article 53(4) ICA gives a person who is appointed as a beneficiary the right to decline this status.

354. Personal insurance regulation contains also a provision concerning the relationships between a policyholder and a beneficiary within a personal insurance contract. In this regard, Article 54 ICA provides that a beneficiary has the right to require from a policyholder, insured person or insurer information on the insurance contract and become acquainted with it.

Article 55 ICA provides regulation on two issues: one relates to elements that should be included in a personal insurance contract indicated in Article 55(1) ICA, and the other to information that should be communicated to the policyholder and the insured if the insurance contract is concluded for a term exceeding one year, such as taxation legal regime and gratuities (bonuses) granted not less than once every twelve months.

Chapter 1. Private Health Insurance

355. Private health insurance is not regulated by the Insurance Contract Act except for few norms. One of such few norms relates to the legal definition of insurable object in respect of personal insurance covering also health as insurable object.[175] Another special norm provides that health insurance is a special type of personal insurance in addition to life insurance and accident insurance.[176]

356. Traditionally, private health insurance in Latvia may be divided into two groups: employers' health insurance and individual health insurance. Health insurance is usually carried out in Latvian insurance market through health insurance contracts concluded by employers for the benefit of their employees. However, in recent years, individual health insurance was commenced by several health insurers in which individual policyholders are able to conclude health insurance contracts independently.

357. Private health insurance contract traditionally includes different kinds of treatment expenses such as visits to a doctor, stay in a hospital, investigations. In addition, other treatment expenses may be covered depending on a private health insurance contract such as dental expenses, massage expenses, expenses concerning physical exercise, rehabilitation.

175. Article 1(7)(c) ICA.
176. Articles 1(20) and 51(1) ICA.

Chapter 2. Accident Insurance

358. The Insurance Contract Act does not provide a specific regulation for accident insurance. Similarly, as in the case of private health insurance discussed above, an exception is provided for characterisation of accident insurance as a type of personal insurance and for the legal definition of insurable object in respect of accident insurance by defining it as 'physical integrity' of a natural person.[177]

Accident insurance contracts are not frequently concluded in Latvia, rather it could be said that few Latvian society members paid attention to this type of insurance and have concluded accident insurance contracts. Therefore, in the case of bodily injuries, Latvian society remains generally uninsured (except for bodily injuries in the case of road traffic accidents covered by motor insurance[178]). As a result, Latvian society members employ other possibilities for compensation of bodily injuries, for instance, by bringing a claim against a tortfeasor if such a person and if his or her civil liability may be established on the basis of delict (non-contractual obligations) law.

177. Articles 1(7)(c), 1(20) and 51(1) ICA.
178. Latvian motor insurance law is discussed above in Part IV.

Chapter 3. Life Insurance

359. Life insurance does not form an exception to the incomplete and fragmented regulation of personal insurance in general and its particular branches such as private health insurance and accident insurance discussed in previous chapters. In effect, different life insurance contract issues such as suicide are left without any statutory regulation, and regulation of these issues is solely left to insurance contract provisions.

360. At the same time, life insurance is subject to special legal norms as regards certain specific life insurance branches that could be offered by life insurers only in addition to life insurance, either in conjuncture with life insurance or separately. However, neither the Insurance Contract Act nor the Insurance and Reinsurance Act provides special regulation for life insurance in general and those specific life insurance types in particular with the exception of provisions that transpose norms of the Solvency II Directive.

361. In this regard, the Insurance and Reinsurance Act provides the division of life insurance into life insurance without saving, life insurance with saving and market-linked life insurance.

362. In addition to the provisions of the Insurance Contract Act and the Insurance and Reinsurance Act discussed above, regulation of life insurance branches is provided by specific binding regulations of the supervisory authority within the course of ensuring supervision of life insurance.

363. Points 4.1 till 4.6 of the normative regulations No 58 of the FKTK 'Normative regulations for the preparation of accounts of insurers and reinsurers' (*Apdrošinātāju un pārapdrošinātāju pārskatu sagatavošanas normatīvie noteikumi* in Latvian) distinguish several life insurance types such as:

- market-linked life insurance – life insurance, in which the policyholder fully or in part assumes investment risk;
- life insurance with saving – life insurance, whose feature is the payment of the insurance sum specified in the contract at the end of the insurance contract or, in case of death of the insured person, if it arises before the expiry of the insurance contract;
- life insurance without saving – life insurance, whose feature is the payment of the insurance sum specified in the insurance contract in the case of death of the insured person during the term of the contract, providing financial protection to those persons who may suffer loss in the event of the death of the insured person during the term of the contract. Life insurance without saving is life insurance for a term, life insurance for the indefinite period (lifetime insurance) and its types;

- lifetime pension insurance – the alternative for utilisation of pension accumulated capital envisaged by Article 7 of the Act on State Funded Pensions,[179] by acquiring a life insurance (lifetime pension) policy[180] with accumulated funded pension capital;
- marriage and child's birth insurance – life insurance, whose feature is the payment of an insurance sum indicated in the contract in the case of marriage and the birth of a child;
- tontines – transactions, by establishing membership associations for the purpose of jointly capitalising contributions and subsequently distributing such accumulated funds to living members of the association or beneficiaries who receive redress in the event of death of the insured.

364. The Insurance Contract Act does not provide any contractual regulation of those life insurance types, except the already- discussed provisions of general regulation of personal insurance. Therefore, insurance contract provisions in respect of those life insurance types fully depend on insurers' offers and contract terms offered (as far as they comply with supervision regulation).

179. Law on State Funded Pensions. The official translation into English is available on the official web page of the Terminology and Translation Centre at http://vvc.gov.lv/image/catalog/dokumenti/Law%20On%20State%20Funded%20Pensions.docx.

180. For lifetime pension, *see* Ch. 5 below.

Chapter 4. Pension Funds

365. Latvian insurance law is familiar with regulation of pension insurance in relation to life insurance to be carried out by life insurers. Two kinds of activities concerning pension insurance may be distinguished: lifetime pension and pension funds relating to participation in a pension fund offered by life insurers. Among insurers, only life insurers may pursue both types of pension insurance, namely to offer concluding a life insurance contract and establishing and managing a pension fund. For each of such activities, a life insurer is obliged to receive a licence as it is envisaged within the supervision of insurance undertakings.[181] The Insurance and Reinsurance Act provides additional rules for those life insurers that are involved in one or both of pension insurance types.

366. Lifetime pension is a specific life insurance type which relates to one of the possibilities for utilisation of the accrued funded pension capital. A participant of the funded pension scheme, upon reaching the age that gives rights to receive the old-age pension or later, has the right to select how he or she will utilise the accrued funded pension capital. Article 7(1) of the Act on State Funded Pensions provides two possibilities: either (1) to add the accrued funded pension capital to the non-funded pension capital and to calculate (recalculate) the old-age pension in accordance with the Law on State Pensions; or (2) to acquire a lifetime pension policy utilising the accrued funded pension capital. In the latter possibility, it is specifically envisaged that '[t]he Cabinet shall issue such standard [regulatory enactments] regarding lifetime assurance'.[182]

367. Lifetime insurance is based on a lifetime insurance contract subject to standard contract terms provided at the legislative level.

368. Formation of the lifetime pension insurance contract is regulated by the regulatory enactment No 272 dated 27 May 2003 of the Cabinet 'Regulatory Enactment for Activity of the state funded pension scheme' in its Chapter VI1 with the title 'Lifetime pension insurance standard terms'.

369. As regards pension funds, they are regulated in Latvia separately on the basis of a special legal act, i.e., Act on Pension Funds.[183] A life insurance company may be one of the persons that may be the founders (stockholders) of an open pension fund (Article 6(2)(2) of the Act on Pension Funds) as well as one of the companies that may hold the funds of the pension scheme (Article 20(1)(2) of the Act on Pension Funds). Additional supervision rules are provided within supervision of life insurance in the Insurance and Reinsurance Act. For instance, an insurer who

181. Article 19(2) (6) and (7) Insurance and Reinsurance Act.
182. Article 7(1)(2) second sentence Act on State Funded Pensions.
183. Law on Private Pension Funds. The official translation into English is available on the official web page of the Terminology and Translation Centre at http://www.vvc.gov.lv/export/sites/default/docs/LRTA/Likumi/On_Private_Pension_Funds.doc.

has received life insurance licence carries out attraction of pension plan participants to a private pension fund as provided by Article 19(1)(4) of the Insurance and Reinsurance Act.

370. If a life insurance company establishes a pension fund, this company drafts a pension plan in accordance with provisions of Article 9 of the Act on Pension Funds and registers it with FKTK. On the basis of the requirements of that Act, participation in a specific pension scheme is a precondition for pension scheme participants to accumulate pension benefits for themselves (Article 10 (1) of the Act on Pension Funds). Pension scheme participants may participate in a pension scheme both directly and through the intermediation of their employers (Article 10 (2) of the Act on Pension Funds).

The Act on Pension Funds provides protection for participants of a pension scheme by providing certain rights for participants of pension schemes envisaged in Article 11 of the Act on Pension Funds and certain guarantees in Article 12 of that Act. In addition, regulation of the Act on Pension Funds provides rules for activity of pension funds, for instance, for their cross-border activity or supervision regulation for their solvency maintenance.

Part VI. Insurance Intermediaries

371. Insurance intermediaries play a considerable role in the insurance market as they are involved in distribution of different insurance products. The same conclusion can be made concerning reinsurance intermediaries as well, yet in narrower meaning due to the specific nature of reinsurance. The regulation of the (re)insurance intermediaries is currently provided in Latvia by the Insurance and Reinsurance Intermediaries Activity Act (also IRIAA). This Act was adopted on 17 March 2005 and entered into force on 15 April 2005. It was amended seven times, the last time in 2017. The Insurance and Reinsurance Intermediaries Activity Act transposes norms of the Insurance Mediation Directive. Currently, the Parliament is considering a draft act for introducing amendments into this Act for transposition of norms of the Insurance Distribution Directive.

Chapter 1. Scope of the Act

372. The Insurance and Reinsurance Intermediaries Activity Act concerns the supervision of both insurance and reinsurance intermediaries. Article 1 of that Act clarifies essential terms used in the regulation of the supervision of both above subjects. Specifically, the term 'insurance intermediary' covers three types of persons that are engaged in insurance mediation for remuneration, i.e., insurance brokers, insurance agents and tied insurance agents (Article 1(3) IRIAA). The term 'insurance mediation' is defined broadly and encompasses all activities concerning the conclusion of an insurance contract (Article 1(1) IRIAA).

At the same time, the term 'reinsurance intermediary' covers one type of persons who are engaged in reinsurance mediation, i.e., reinsurance brokers (Article 1(4) IRIAA). In addition, the term 'reinsurance mediation' is defined similarly as the term 'insurance mediation' mentioned in the previous paragraph, yet in relation to conclusion of a reinsurance contract (Article 1(2) IRIAA).

The Insurance and Reinsurance Intermediaries Activity Act applies also to EU insurance intermediaries and EU reinsurance intermediaries who employ either freedom of establishment or freedom to provide services. Their activities are regulated separately in Chapter VI of the Insurance and Reinsurance Intermediaries Activity Act.

Chapter 2. Supervision Activities

373. There could be distinguished several supervision activities in respect of insurance intermediaries and reinsurance intermediaries. The first supervision activity refers to registration of insurance and reinsurance intermediaries. Registration of insurance brokers and insurance agents as well as reinsurance brokers (all together referred to as registrable subjects) is carried out in the insurance and reinsurance intermediary register. This register is maintained by FKTK who is the supervision authority also for insurers and reinsurers as discussed previously. Insurance brokers maintain their own registers of their employees engaged in insurance intermediation. Each insurance agent maintains its own tied insurance intermediary register whose registration regulation is provided separately on the basis of Chapter IV of the Insurance and Reinsurance Intermediaries Activity Act.

374. The registration requirements are provided in Chapter II of the Insurance and Reinsurance Intermediaries Activity Act covering legal forms that could be used by registrable subjects; information that should be recorded in the insurance and reinsurance intermediary register; and requirements for registration in that register.

375. Another supervision activity covers compulsory civil liability insurance of registrable subjects that is regulated in Chapter III of the Insurance and Reinsurance Intermediaries Activity Act.

376. The relationships between insurance intermediaries or reinsurance intermediaries with their clients are regulated separately in Chapter V of the Insurance and Reinsurance Intermediaries Activity Act. Article 23(1) of the Insurance and Reinsurance Intermediaries Activity Act prescribes a lawful standard of care to be ensured by insurance and reinsurance intermediaries referring to the criterion of an honest and careful proprietor in order to provide insurance and reinsurance mediation with the appropriate professionalism and care.

377. The information that must be submitted to the client is provided in Articles 24–27 IRIAA.

378. One of the most important (perhaps even the most important) supervision aspects of insurance mediation relates to protection of policyholders and persons that may claim insurance redress. By choosing one of the options provided by the Insurance Mediation Directive, Article 28 of the Insurance and Reinsurance Intermediaries Activity Act provides the following rule:

> An insurance premium payment made in accordance with an insurance contract, which is paid by a customer to an insurance intermediary, shall be treated in any case as a payment made to an insurance undertaking or a branch of a non-Member-State insurer, whereas a payment made by an insurance merchant or by a branch of a non-Member-State insurer to an insurance intermediary shall not be treated as a payment made to a customer until the customer actually receives the monies.

This provision was subject to interpretation given by the Latvian Supreme Court in a case. In this case, a policyholder paid the insurance premium to the insurance broker who did not forward this insurance premium to the insurer. The insurer raised a claim for payment of insurance premium against the policyholder but not against the insurance broker. The Latvian Supreme Court refused this claim by establishing that the payment of an insurance premium paid to the insurance broker establishes the fact of the fulfilment of obligation of the payment of the insurance premium on the basis of the discussed provision.[184]

184. Judgment of the Latvian Supreme Court dated 21 Jun. 2016 in Case No SKC-63/2016.

Chapter 3. Scope of Supervision

379. Supervision scope is regulated in Chapter V of the Insurance and Reinsurance Intermediaries Activity Act. This chapter provides that the FKTK is the supervision authority for the supervision of insurance and reinsurance mediation. This chapter lays down state duties for registration and provides competence for the above state institution.

Part VII. Reinsurance and Co-insurance

Chapter 1. Reinsurance

380. Reinsurance plays an important role in the distribution of risks among society and disallows the situation that the insurer alone undertakes insurance of accepted insured risks in respect of all or certain types of insurance contracts. Reinsurance is treated as a special type of insurance requiring a special licence, and it is based on a special contract called a reinsurance contract. Reinsurance is usually subject to specific regulation regarding supervision; however, it is rarely regulated concerning contractual matters.

381. In Latvia, regulation of reinsurance is envisaged in the Insurance and Reinsurance Act only from the supervision point of view. At the same time, contractual matters are not, and even cannot be, regulated by the Insurance and Reinsurance Act as this Act covers supervision (yet, as discussed above, it still includes regulation of certain contractual aspects but only in relation to insurance contracts but not to reinsurance contracts). Likewise, regulation of reinsurance contracts is explicitly excluded from the scope of general insurance contract regulation contained in the Insurance Contract Act.

382. The legal definition of reinsurance is included in the Insurance and Reinsurance Act. Article 1(2) of this Act defines reinsurance as 'acceptance of the ceded risks from the insurance merchant, reinsurance merchant or private pension fund'. Likewise, the Insurance and Reinsurance Act defines the term of retrocession being similar to reinsurance. Article 1(4) of that Act defines retrocession as 'assignment of reinsured risks to an insurance or reinsurance undertaking'.

383. As regards supervision of reinsurance, reinsurers are subject to general regulation of supervision and specific regulation in respect of reinsurance supervision. Both these types of regulation are included in the Insurance and Reinsurance Act.

Contractual matters of reinsurance contracts are solely based on reinsurance contract provisions, yet subject to general regulation of the law of obligations contained in the Latvian Civil Act and within the limits allowed for reinsurers from their supervision point of view. Such lack of specific regulation for reinsurance contracts in Latvian insurance contract law means that the reinsurance contract is subject to general regulation of contract formation; form requirements which are liberally regulated in Latvian contract law; termination of the reinsurance obligation, including the general term of limitation period. Likewise, regulation of reinsurance contract and its problem issues is almost undiscussed in Latvian insurance law literature with the exception of some fragmentary aspects. In addition, as far as the anonymised database of court practice of Latvian courts is concerned, there are no court cases involving disputes over reinsurance contracts dealt by Latvian courts.

Chapter 2. Co-insurance

384. Co-insurance plays an important role for situations when one insurer is not capable or unwilling to insure a particular insurance object against one or several insurable risks in question. Co-insurance may be subject to specific regulation both from the point of view of supervision and contract law. Latvia provides regulation for both of these regulatory aspects of co-insurance.

385. As regards supervision, the Insurance and Reinsurance Act in its Chapter XXIII provides specific regulation for co-insurance supervision by transposing norms from the Solvency II Directive in respect of Community co-insurance operations.[185] However, co-insurance supervision rules included in Chapter XXIII of the Insurance and Reinsurance Act are fragmentary as they relate to the calculation of technical reserves[186] and the exchange of information of insurance supervisors from respective EU Member States.[187]

386. Contractual matters are regulated in a specific chapter in the Insurance Contract Act, namely Chapter VI of that Act (Articles 33–34 ICA). As it may be concluded from the regulation included in this Chapter to be discussed further, it cannot be considered as comprehensive but rather as fragmentary and obviously incomplete.

387. Regulation of co-insurance contractual aspects is included in Chapter VI of the Insurance Contract Act. This regulation envisages general regulation of co-insurance (Article 33 ICA) and two specific elements in Article 34 ICA, namely, communication between a policyholder and the leading insurer (Article 34 (2) and (3) ICA), on the one hand, and relationships between the leading insurer and an co-insurer or co-insurers (Article 34 (1) ICA), on the other.

388. Article 33 ICA provides general regulation of co-insurance which is as follows:

> [I]n co-insurance all insurers who enter into an insurance contract shall sign an insurance contract. Rights and duties of the parties shall be determined in conformity with the insurance contract. If in the insurance contract there is no special agreement between insurers, co-insurance shall not create full (joint) liability of the insurers.

389. As one may observe from this Article, it contains three different legal norms in each sentence. The first sentence of Article 33 ICA provides that a leading co-insurer and co-insurers conclude a co-insurance contract. The elements of the

185. Articles 190–196 Solvency II Directive.
186. Article 184 Insurance and Reinsurance Act.
187. Article 187 Insurance and Reinsurance Act.

co-insurance contract are not specifically regulated. In this situation, the second sentence of Article 33 ICA on regulation of rights and duties just establishes the obvious fact that the contractual relationship arising from co-insurance is not regulated by this Act. The third sentence of Article 33 ICA is related to the essence of an obligation upon which the co-insurance relationship is based. This provision provides that a co-insurance obligation in Latvian insurance contract law is treated as a shared obligation but not a joint obligation. In this regard, this provision is linked with the general regulation of law of obligations which, inter alia, concerns the division of obligations into shared (divisible) and joint obligations. As regards both types of obligations, Article 1669 of the Civil Act states that:

> If more than one person from one or the other side or from both sides participate in an obligation right, then the claim and relevant obligations thereto shall be either several, such that each creditor may claim only his or her own part of the subject-matter and each debtor must perform only his or her own part of the obligation, or joint.

390. In the co-insurance context, this provision means that an insured may bring a claim against a leading co-insurer and all co-insurers in a proportional manner by requesting to collect a proportionate part of the amount of insurance redress from each of them, but not insurance redress in full from each of these persons.

Chapter 3. Insurance Pools

391. A specific kind of co-insurance relates to insurance pools. An insurance pool comprises a permanently acting group of insurers who jointly insure a separate insurable risk or insurable risks falling within a separate insurance class (insurance type). Currently, Latvian insurance market is not familiar with any insurance pool operating in Latvia as there is no such insurance pool established by Latvian insurers. Such situation may be explained by the relatively small size of Latvian insurance market and lack or low possibility of serious insurable risks in Latvia which would require the use of an insurance pool. However, such a situation does not mean that Latvian policyholders may not take a possibility to conclude an insurance contract with an insurance pool operating abroad.

Part VIII. Taxation of Insurance

392. Taxation plays significant role in insurance market both in relation to taxation of insurers and insurance and reinsurance intermediaries, on the one hand, and policyholders and insured persons, on the other. Latvian law does not envisage a special legal act for the taxation regulation concerning insurance matters. However, special legal norms concerning insurance matters are provided by tax law regulation, yet these norms are scattered among different provisions in different tax legal acts.

In this situation, one may distinguish three types of taxes which directly or indirectly are related to insurance contract relationships, i.e., value added tax, income tax in relation to natural persons and income tax in relation to undertakings and self-employed persons.

Chapter 1. Value Added Tax

393. Regulation of value added tax is provided by the Value Added Tax Act,[188] which covers certain aspects concerning insurance legal relationships. One of the main provisions in the Value Added Tax Act in respect of insurance contract relationships concerns exemptions from application of value added tax which, inter alia, covers also insurance and reinsurance services, i.e., (re)insurance premiums and remuneration of (re)insurance intermediaries in accordance with provisions of the Value Added Tax Act. This specific exemption concerning (re)insurance premiums and remuneration of (re)insurance intermediaries is included in Article 52(1)(20) of the Value Added Tax Act which provides that value added tax is not applied, inter alia, in respect of such supplies of goods and services:

> [I]nsurance and reinsurance services in accordance with the Law On Insurance Companies and Supervision Thereof [the Value Added Tax Act still contains the reference to the previously effective Act, now it is replaced by the Insurance and Reinsurance Act – author's remark], as well as insurance and reinsurance intermediary services in accordance with the Activities of Insurance and Reinsurance Intermediaries Law.

394. Likewise, this exemption is provided also in another situation concerning insurers, i.e., in case if services which are related to the management of insurance companies' portfolios.[189]

395. Furthermore, other provisions included in the Value Added Tax Act relate to insurance relationships in certain cases. Indeed, special norms in relation to establishing the place of provision of services in relation to insurance are provided separately.[190] Also, the value of supply of goods also includes all expenses, inter alia, in relation to insurance.[191] Likewise, in the case of importation of goods, different types of costs, such as insurance costs incurred until the first destination in inland, shall be added to the customs value of imported goods unless the value of such services is already included in that customs value.[192]

In addition, special rules in respect of insurance legal relationships are provided in the case of special tax application arrangement in transactions with second-hand goods, works of art, collectors' items and antiques in accordance with Article 138 of the Value Added Tax Act.

---

188. Value Added Tax Law. The official translation into English is available on the official web page of the Terminology and Translation Centre at http://vvc.gov.lv/image/catalog/dokumenti/Value%20Added%20Tax%20Law.docx.
189. Article 52(1)(22) Value Added Tax Act.
190. Article 30(1)(9) Value Added Tax Act.
191. Article 35(1) Value Added Tax Act.
192. Article 36(1) Value Added Tax Act.

Chapter 2. Personal Income Tax

396. Specific rules in relation to insurance legal relationships are provided also in the case of personal income tax for natural persons regulated by the Personal Income Tax Act.[193]

397. The Personal Income Tax Act does not envisage that insurance redress shall be qualified as a taxable income and, therefore, insurance redress is not subject to application of personal income tax. An exception exists in the case of three situations provided both for Latvian taxpayers (i.e., residents) and non-Latvian taxpayers (i.e., non-residents), namely:

- insurance compensation which in accordance with personal insurance contract entered into by the employer (or another policyholder – legal person) is paid out when the end of the time period provided in the contract has come or when terminating the contract before the time period in the interests of the insured;
- income from life insurance contracts entered into with an accumulation of funds;
- income from lifetime pension insurance contract which is formed from gratifications granted by an insurer.[194]

398. Furthermore, annual taxable income does not cover and, therefore, certain income types related to insurance redress are released from payment of this tax. These income types are as follows.

399. First, Article 9 of the Personal Income Tax Act provides that insurance redress is not covered by annual taxable income with *three exceptions*. These three exceptions relate to the first and third situations discussed above,[195] but the third exception concerns disbursed insurance compensations, if the insurance premium has been included in the economic activity expenditure of the payer.[196]

400. Second, compensations for personified expenditure in relation to volunteering which, in accordance with provisions of a volunteering agreement, shall be covered for a volunteer by organisers of volunteering for health and life insurance against accidents during volunteering or for civil liability insurance against third parties (except for motor insurance).[197]

193. Law 'On Personal Income Tax'. The official translation into English is available on the official web page of the Terminology and Translation Centre at http://vvc.gov.lv/image/catalog/dokumenti/On%20Personal%20Income%20Tax.docx.
194. Articles 3(3)(13), (22) and (23) Personal Income Tax Act (non-residents); Arts 8 (3)(20) and (20.1), Art. 8 (5)–(5.2) and 8(13) (residents).
195. Article 9(1)(4)–(4.1) Personal Income Tax Act.
196. Article 9(3.4) Personal Income Tax Act.
197. Article 9 (1)(44)b)–c) Personal Income Tax Act.

401. In addition, eligible expenditure, i.e., expenditure of the tax payer that shall be deducted from the amount of annual taxable income, includes, inter alia, payments of health insurance premiums of the tax payer and members of his or her family, and payments of insurance premiums made in conformity with a life insurance contract (with accumulation of funds) within certain amounts.[198]

402. Important regulation concerns payments that are made in relation to insurance which may be included in the expenditure related to acquiring income in the taxation year from economic activity. Two payments in relation to insurance are included in this expenditure, i.e., the premium amounts for life assurance (with accumulation of funds) and the premium amounts paid into private pension funds in conformity with licensed pension plans and life, health and accident insurance (without accumulation of funds) paid in for employees as well as payment of mandatory insurance premiums for the fixed assets used in economic activities.[199]

In addition, the Personal Income Tax Act provides special rules for other issues by touching different insurance aspects such as concerning different types of income, the date of obtaining income, payment of tax and other issues.

198. Article 10 (1)(2)–(6) in conjuncture with Art. 10(6)–(8) Personal Income Tax Act.
199. Article 11(3) (7)–(71) Personal Income Tax Act.

Chapter 3. Enterprise Income Tax

403. Specific rules are provided in relation to enterprise income tax whose regulation is provided for in the Enterprise Income Tax.[200] Taxable income of a taxpayer shall be increased by, inter alia, payments made by the employer for the benefit of employees into private pension funds and paid in amounts of insurance premiums for employee life insurance (with savings funds).[201] Likewise, in determining taxable income, the profit of a taxpayer (subject to tax) may be reduced by payments of insurance premiums.[202]

404. A specific provision is provided for establishing the value of a representation passenger car if it is leased without the right of purchase – the value of the passenger car if it is not indicated in the leasing contract is the value of the car indicated in the insurance contract of the car.[203]

405. In addition, Article 8 of the Enterprise Income Tax Act provides regulation for funds intended for technical reserves of insurance and reinsurance companies by providing that taxable income of insurance and reinsurance companies shall not be increased by such amount of deductions which has been included in technical reserves and shall not be reduced by the amount withdrawn from such reserves and included in the income.

200. Law 'On Enterprise Income Tax'. The official translation into English is available on the official web page of the Terminology and Translation Centre at http://vvc.gov.lv/image/catalog/dokumenti/Enterprise%20Income%20Tax.docx.
201. Article 6(1)(12) Enterprise Income Tax Act.
202. Article 6(6) Enterprise Income Tax Act.
203. Article 6.5(3) Enterprise Income Tax Act.

Part IX. Risk Management and Prevention

406. Risk management and prevention plays a considerable role in insurance economics, on the one hand, and regulation of insurance, on the other. Risk management and prevention is provided in Latvian insurance law through supervision of insurance as discussed above. At the same time, a special role in risk management and prevention is played by funds which secure that victims exposed to occurrence of certain risks will be compensated for damages caused. Two funds are provided by Latvian insurance law for avoiding the damage caused by certain risks such as insolvency of insurers or certain drivers in road traffic accidents are not left uncompensated. Both these funds are treated separately, and their regulation is included in specific legal acts. Another fund is provided within regulation of medical treatment for covering damage caused to patients within the course of medical treatment. These funds will be discussed separately within next chapters of this Part of the monograph.

Chapter 1. Guarantee Fund Within Motor Insurance

407. A special fund is provided in *motor insurance* to prevent a risk for non-compensation of damage caused to victims of road traffic accidents. The most important situations exist in the case if damage is caused by a liable motor vehicle driver who is either *uninsured or unidentified* (the so-called hit-and-run). For prevention of the risk that victims of the road traffic accidents are left without compensation for the damage caused, the Guarantee Fund is established in accordance with provisions of the Motor Insurance Act in conjuncture with EU motor insurance law. This fund is operated by the Latvian national insurers' bureau, i.e., Motor Insurers' Bureau of Latvia established in the form of a society. Regulation of activity of the Latvian national insurers' bureau is provided by Part IV of the Motor Insurance Act which inter alia envisages rules in respect of the Guarantee Fund in Articles 51 and 51.[1] of that Act.

408. Money accumulated in the Guarantee fund is mainly collected as deductions from each insurance premium paid within a motor insurance contract, however other incomes are possible as provided by Article 51(6) of the Motor Insurance Act in conjuncture with a separate regulatory enactment of the Cabinet. The operation of the Guarantee fund is entrusted to the Latvian national insurers' bureau (Article 51(7) of the Motor Insurance Act) within the procedure prescribed by the Motor Insurance Act. Payment of insurance redress from this fund takes place if the Latvian national insurers' bureau establishes one of situations when the payment is permitted from the Guarantee fund – the exhaustive list of these cases is included in Article 51(1) of the Motor Insurance Act. The most important cases, as it was already noted above, are two, i.e. damage is caused to a victim of a road traffic accident by either an uninsured or an unidentified motor vehicle driver.

409. If damage is caused by the uninsured motor vehicle driver, the Latvian national insurers' bureau is entitled to bring a recourse (subrogation) claim against the owner or the lawful user of the motor vehicle in question in the full amount of insurance redress paid to the victim. Such recourse (subrogation) claims are frequently reviewed by Latvian courts and usually satisfied (and usually not appealed at an appeal instance).

The reason for the occurrence of such claims against the owner or the lawful user of a motor vehicle which were driven by a liable uninsured motor vehicle driver is not always related to intentional avoiding from conclusion of a motor insurance contract. Rather this situation is related to a lack of knowledge of termination of a motor insurance contract among Latvian society members. One of the most frequent (perhaps even the most frequent) grounds for termination of a motor insurance contract relates to either alienation of a motor vehicle or registration of the new acquirer of a motor vehicle (Article 10(1)(1) of the Motor Insurance Act). Both of these termination grounds are unknown to many members of Latvian society who may not conclude a motor insurance contract immediately after either acquiring of a motor vehicle or its subsequent registration as they assume that the motor insurance contract concluded by the previous owner still continues to operate. As a result, if a new owner of a motor vehicle himself or herself or another driver whom that vehicle was handed over does not conclude a motor insurance contract after acquiring the vehicle, any of these drivers are considered as uninsured.

Chapter 2. Insured Protection Fund

410. Another fund prevents a risk that persons having claims against insurers will be left without their fulfilment in the case of *insolvency* of an insurer. This fund is called Insured Protection Fund and is regulated in Chapter XXXVIII (Articles 283–290) of the Insurance and Reinsurance Act.

411. Accumulation of money in this fund is formed on the basis of deduction in the amount of 1% of the total amount of gross insurance premiums in certain insurance types as well as other incomes in relation to this money (penalties for late payment of these deductions; income from investment of monies accumulated in this fund; etc). This fund is operated by FKTK. However, the above Act allows to transfer an operation right of this fund to another person if that Commission decides so.

412. However, prevention of risk of insolvency of insurers is *seriously damaged* by *a set of limitations* for claims that are satisfied from the Insured Protection Fund. Chapter XXXVIII of the Insurance and Reinsurance Act provides these limitations which are as follows.

413. The first limitation relates to time moment when a claim may be submitted to the Insured Protection Fund. Satisfying a claim from this fund is possible only after insolvency of a Latvian insurer or a Member State insurer is declared; it is established that there are no financial means to fulfil those claims which are to be compensated by this fund (these claims are discussed below); and there is a list of claims drafted and submitted by the insolvency administrator of an insurer in question.[204]

414. Another limitation covers subjects who may submit the claim: only if an insured is a natural person, insurance redress on the basis of an insurance contract concluded by that person may be claimed from this fund.[205] It should be admitted that by a mistake a respective provision refers to a policyholder but not the insured. However, as it arises from the nature of wording of respective provisions related to payment of insurance redress from the Insured Protection Fund, an insured is actually meant as a creditor for claims from this fund but not the policyholder. From the point of view of the Insurance and Reinsurance Act, this natural person may cover both consumers and non-consumers

415. The third limitation relates to the type of claims to be compensated. The position of Latvian insurance law traditionally was related to the fact that only insurance redress should be compensated from this fund as such approach was also employed by the previously effective Act. Therefore, the current as well as the previous legal act on insurance supervision do not allow compensation of claims

204. Article 290 Insurance and Reinsurance Act.
205. Article 285(1) Insurance and Reinsurance Act.

against an insurer other than claim for payment of insurance redress such as collection of insurance premiums, damages, interest.[206]

416. An exception relates to claims against insolvent mutual insurance cooperative companies, which are excluded from compensation from the Insured Protection Fund.[207]

417. The last – fourth – limitation relates to the amount of insurance redress to be paid which is differentiated depending on the fact whether insurance redress is a claim on the basis of a non-life or life insurance contract.

418. In the case of non-life insurance, insurance redress may be claimed in the amount of 50% but not more than EUR 3000 for each of the insured (the Act mistakenly refers to a policyholder as noted above) and only in relation to specific non-life insurance types (accident insurance, health insurance, motor vehicle insurance except railway transport, property insurance, motor insurance, general civil liability insurance and assistance insurance).[208]

419. As regards life insurance, insurance redress may be claimed in the amount of 100% but not more than EUR 15,000 for each of the insured (the Act mistakenly refers to a policyholder) and only in relation to all life insurance types in which a licence shall be obtained except market-linked life insurance.[209]

420. As one may observe from overview of these limitations, regulation of claims to be compensated from the Insured Protection Fund is incomplete and even discriminatory as only natural persons are covered; however, legal persons are also in the same situation, and only certain claims are compensated in a certain amount which does not correspond to the interests of civil circulation.

206. *Ibid.*
207. Article 286(1) Insurance and Reinsurance Act.
208. Article 285(1)(2) Insurance and Reinsurance Act.
209. Article 285(1)(1) Insurance and Reinsurance Act.

Chapter 3. Medical Treatment Risk Fund

421. As it was noted above regarding compulsory insurance,[210] the Latvian legislature has chosen to abandon compulsory insurance for *doctors* concerning medical treatment activity by replacing that compulsory insurance with establishing a special fund which is named as the Medical Treatment Risk Fund.

The legal status of the Medical Treatment Risk Fund is governed by Article 17 of the Patient Rights Act.[211] Particularly, Article 17(3) of that Act provides that the amount of medical treatment risk payment to be paid annually by medical treatment institutions and procedure for its payment are set out in a separate regulatory enactment of the Cabinet. However, regulation of compensation amount and grounds for payment of compensation are regulated by Article 16 of the Patient Rights Act in conjuncture with a separate regulatory enactment of the Cabinet which provides procedure for submitting a claim for compensation from this fund. Medical institutions make contributions to this fund, and compensation is provided to victims from the money accumulated within that fund for damage caused during medical treatment. Article 16(2) of the Patient Rights Act provides that the maximum amount of compensation for damage to patient's life or health cannot exceed EUR 142,290, but for compensation of medical treatment expenses, not more than EUR 28,460.

422. According to publicly available information, patients have been paid compensation from the Medical Treatment Risk Fund during its first four years of activity amounting to more than EUR 3.5 million, including two patients who received compensation in the maximum possible amount, i.e., EUR 142,000 (currently EUR 142,290).[212] The most frequent cases for payment of compensation relate to civil liability for medical treatment in traumatology, neurology, surgery and gynaecology.[213]

---

210. *See* General Introduction, §7 of this monograph above.
211. Law On the Rights of Patients. The official translation into English is available on the official web page of the Terminology and Translation Centre at http://vvc.gov.lv/export/sites/default/docs/LRTA/Likumi/Law_On_the_Rights_of_Patients.doc.
212. TVNET, 2018. gada 04. janvāris. Available in Latvian at http://www.tvnet.lv/zinas/latvija/767387-par_arstu_kludam_142000.
213. *Ibid.*

Selected Bibliography

Please note that bibliography sources indicated in this chapter contain only sources on Latvian insurance law published in English.

Kārkliņš J., Mantrov V. Company Law and Insolvency Law, in: Tanel Kerikmäe, Kristi Joamets, Jānis Pleps, Anita Rodiņa, Tomas Berkmanas, Edita Gruodytė (eds). The Law of the Baltic States. Cham: Springer, 2017, pp. 304–320.

Mantrov V. Perception of Insurable Interest in European Insurance Law. Latvijas Universitātes žurnāls 'Juridiskā zinātne'/Journal of the University of Latvia 'Law', 2017, No. 10, pp. 248–267.

Mantrov V. Problem Questions of Insurance Contract Regulation in Latvia. The Quality of Legal Acts and Its Importance in Contemporary Legal Space, Collection of Research Papers Presented During the International Scientific Conference, 4–5 October 2012 at the University of Latvia Faculty of Law, Riga (University of Latvia, Riga 2012), pp. 562–574.

Mantrov V. Regulation of Recourse Claim Grounds in Latvian Motor Insurance Law, in: Constitutional Values in Contemporary Legal Space II, 16–17 November, 2016: Collection of Research Papers. Riga: University of Latvia Press, 2016, pp. 278–293.

Mantrov V. Is 142 Euro Equal to 350 000 Euro? The CJEU Interpretation of 'Personal Injury' and 'Injured Party' in: EU Motor Insurance Law. *European Journal of Risk Regulation*, 2014, pp. 399–406.

Torgāns K. Saistību tiesības. Mācību grāmata. R.: Tiesu namu aģentūra, 2014, 453–455.lpp.; Torgāns K. Regresa prasība OCTA apdrošināšanā. Civiltiesību, komerctiesību un civilprocesa aktualitātes: raksti, 1999–2008. Current topics on civil, commercial law and civil procedure: selected articles, 1999–2008. R.: Tiesu namu aģentūra, 2009, 567–583.lpp.

Torgāns K., Kārkliņš J. Contract Law, in: Tanel Kerikmäe, Kristi Joamets, Jānis Pleps, Anita Rodiņa, Tomas Berkmanas, Edita Gruodytė (eds). The Law of the Baltic States. Cham: Springer, 2017, pp. 291–304.

Index

The numbers below refer to paragraph numbers.

Index

Index

Made in the USA
Monee, IL
18 October 2026

66041411R10090